Heaven
on
Earth

Heaven
on
Earth

LIVING *in the* FULLNESS *of* GOD'S KINGDOM HERE *and* NOW

EUGENE H. LOWE, PH.D.

PUBLISHING & MARKETING

Orlando, Florida

Heaven on Earth–Living in the Fullness of God's Kingdom Here and Now
By: Eugene H. Lowe

Published by HigherLife
Development Services, Inc.
PO Box 623307
Oviedo, FL 32762
407-563-4806
www.ahigherlife.com

All Scripture quotations are taken from the New American Standard Bible®, copyright © 1960, 1962, 1963, 1968, 1971, 1973, 1975, 1977, 1995 by The Lockman Foundation. Used by permission. (www.Lockman.org)

ISBN 13: 978-1-939183-99-6
ISBN-10:1-939183-99-5

Cover Design: Judith McKittrick Wright

First Edition

10 11 12 13 — 9 8 7 6 5 4 3 2 1

Printed in the United States of America

CONTENTS

Section 3: God Desires Intimate Fellowship with Us

Section 4: How Should We Treat Fellow Citizens of God's Kingdom?

INTRODUCTION

How might we describe the kingdom of God? We can define it as his kingship and everything that his kingship involves. That includes his power, his authority, his domain, and his subjects. His power is unlimited: he is Almighty God. His authority is absolute: he alone is sovereign. His domain encompasses all of heaven and earth. His subjects include the angels and all of mankind. God's kingdom incorporates everything that is, everything that has been, and everything that will be, whether it is something physical or spiritual, and whether it is located within or outside of our universe. All of it is part of God's creation. He is the king over everything, everywhere, forever.

Because God's domain includes the earth, everyone lives within his kingdom. Whether or not we realize it or fully appreciate it, each of us continually experiences joys, blessings, and privileges from living in God's kingdom. There is the joy of encountering an old friend or making a new one. There are places we can visit to experience the beauty and majesty of nature. And perhaps best of all, we have the privilege of unlimited access to God in prayer. As we gain new insights into God's kingdom and all that it means to us here and now, we can acquire a greater vision and purpose for our lives.

The kingdom of God is one of the most frequently mentioned subjects in the Bible, yet it can seem complex and difficult to understand. One reason is that the Bible is not organized topically. Instead, information about most topics is spread throughout it in a variety of ways and contexts. This book will help you to understand the seven most important topics related to living in the kingdom of God. We will begin in section 1 with a brief history of the kingdom from creation to the coming of Christ. This will give us a better appreciation of the reality and purpose of God's kingdom.

People have many diverse ideas about God and what he is like. Suppose we were to delineate the characteristics we would like him to have. What would that list look like? How closely would it conform to what he is really like? We will discuss that in section 2.

Section 3 introduces our relationship with God. In the same way that living in a country does not automatically make someone a citizen of that country, living on the earth does not automatically make someone a citizen of God's kingdom. A prerequisite of citizenship and its privileges is that a person voluntarily establishes a relationship with God. He allows us to control how distant or intimate we want that relationship to be. But the closer we draw to him, the more fully we can enjoy the incredible blessings and privileges that he makes available to us.

Our relationships with God and with people are the most important aspects of living here and now in the kingdom of God. In section 4 we will address what our attitude and behavior should be toward our fellow citizens of God's kingdom. Jesus summarized it well when he said that we should love one another. We will look in some depth at what that entails. Jesus also said that we should love our neighbors as much as we love ourselves. Based on that, in section 5 we will investigate how to treat people who are not yet citizens of God's kingdom.

Section 6 explains why Jesus was uniquely qualified to speak authoritatively about the kingdom of God. First, he was relating what he had seen and done while he dwelled in heaven before coming to earth. Second, he was revealing what he would do when he returned to his place in heaven, which would include reigning over the kingdom of God.

During Jesus' teaching ministry on earth, he focused on the kingdom of God, revealing and explaining the key principles by which it operates. He did that because the Father and he knew that, to the degree that we understand and adhere to those principles, our lives will be more fulfilled and enriched, and we will have a greater impact for good upon the people with whom we come into contact. In section 7, we will explore those key principles.

My hope for you is that this book will enable you to better understand and more fully appreciate the wonderful blessings and privileges, as well as the companion responsibilities, we have as citizens of God's kingdom.

Section 1:

A BRIEF HISTORY OF GOD'S KINGDOM ON EARTH

INTRODUCTION

In this section we will seek to better understand and put into perspective the history of God's kingdom from its beginning until the coming of Christ. We will focus on God's interactions with key individuals and with the nation of Israel.

THE ORIGIN OF GOD'S KINGDOM

When did the kingdom of God begin? It predates the universe. It existed before the creation of angels and the other heavenly beings, and long before the creation of the earth and we who dwell upon it. God's kingdom is an eternal kingdom. Like God himself, his kingdom had no beginning and it will never cease to be.

The Lord is King forever and ever [Psalm 10:16a].

Your kingdom is an everlasting kingdom, and Your dominion endures throughout all generations [Psalm 145:13].

CREATION

Scientists, using data they accumulated and analyzed from many sources, calculate that the universe began as an enormous explosion sometime between 13.5 and 13.9 billion years ago. It seems preposterous to assert that this was a completely random event and that all that substance—energy, matter, and/or something else—spontaneously created itself. If such an explanation were valid, why did it never happen before? And why has it not happened again, even on a much-reduced scale? As the universe continues to expand, what does it expand into? Where did all that empty space come from?

Rather than creation being merely a fortunate-for-us, spontaneous event, the Bible teaches that everything came into being by an act of God. It was he who set the universe's physical processes into motion and created the heavens that we see around us and the earth upon which we live.

In the beginning God created the heavens and the earth [Genesis 1:1].

You alone are the Lord.
You have made the heavens,
The heaven of heavens with all their host,
The earth and all that is on it,
The seas and all that is in them.
You give life to all of them
And the heavenly host bows down before You
[Nehemiah 9:6].

Thus says the Lord, the Holy One of Israel...
"It is I who made the earth, and created man upon it.
I stretched out the heavens with My hands
And I ordained all their host"
[Isaiah 45:11a, 12].

God saw all that He had made, and behold, it was very good [Genesis 1:31a].

Have you, like me, been awestruck by the beauty and magnificence of the stars on a clear dark night? At such a time we can readily identify with David when he wrote,

The heavens are telling of the glory of God;
And their expanse is declaring the work of His hands [Psalm 19:1].

With our unaided eyes we can see a few thousand of the perhaps 200 to 400 billion stars in our Milky Way galaxy. Our galaxy is so vast that it takes light, moving at 5.6 trillion miles a year, approximately 100,000 years to traverse its diameter. Yet the dimensions of the Milky Way are minuscule compared to those of the universe.

Recent data from the Hubble and other telescopes indicates that the universe contains on the order of 125 billion galaxies. A typical galaxy contains several billion stars, although dwarf galaxies can have as few as 10 million and giant galaxies can have a trillion. God's kingdom extends throughout the entire universe. Isn't God awesome! And doesn't the vast-ness of the universe make us feel infinitesimally small?

> When I consider Your heavens, the work of Your fingers,
> The moon and the stars, which You have ordained;
> What is man that You take thought of him,
> And the son of man that You care for him? [Psalm 8:3–4].

What a question! Why would such a magnificent, Almighty God take notice of us? And yet, as the psalmist wrote, God is attentive to even the smallest details of our lives.

> O Lord, You have searched me and known me.
> You know when I sit down and when I rise up;
> You understand my thought from afar.
> You scrutinize my path and my lying down,
> And are intimately acquainted with all my ways.
> Even before there is a word on my tongue,
> Behold, O Lord, You know it all.
> You have enclosed me behind and before,
> And laid Your hand upon me.
> Such knowledge is too wonderful for me;
> It is too high, I cannot attain to it
> [Psalm 139:1–6].

Yes, the Bible assures us that God knows us intimately, loves us deeply, watches over us unfailingly, and is always accessible to us in prayer.

One time when my wife Brenda and I were discussing creation, she recalled visiting the home of a friend who had three young children. She had noticed that everything in that home was focused on the children. The parents delighted to be able to provide them with a safe, nurturing, fun, and educationally enriching environment. The earth is like that. God has provided us with a safe, nurturing, fun, and educationally enriching envi-ronment in which to live, work, and enjoy life.

My father's hobby was raising chickens. I don't mean fryers and hens and eggs for eating. He raised Bantam show chickens. Breeding and showing them for prizes was a great love of his. His favorite variety was the Cornish game, but I also remember him having white, buff, and black Cochins that have feathers on their legs, as well as gold and silver Sebrights. Can you imagine God's delight that Henry Lowe appreciated the beauty and variety of chickens? How many people appreciate chickens other than as food? It's definitely a small group.

Our son Jake was intellectually precocious, learning to read long before he entered school. When he lost his first tooth, Brenda took on the role of the tooth fairy. Instead of slipping money under his pillow while he slept, she decided to make it a game—a treasure hunt. She put a note under his pillow that pointed him to the first clue. A note there directed him to another clue. To our surprise, not only did he not enter into the fun and adventure of the game, he was both disappointed and angry because he had already read about what the tooth fairy should do, and the treasure hunt did not meet his expectations. Don't we sometimes behave like that, becoming disappointed and angry when circumstances, people's actions, or events do not conform to our expectations? As a result, we often miss out on adventures, delights, or learning opportunities that God has prepared for us. Let's open ourselves up to enjoy and appreciate more of the experiences that God sends our way.

1-4

COMPETING SUPPOSITIONS THAT PEOPLE HOLD CONCERNING CREATION

God created and custom-tailored the earth for our benefit. He is always present, working invisibly behind the scenes of our lives. But people hold diverse ideas about God, creation, and his degree of involvement in the universe and with us. Each of those ideas carries with it certain implications about how we ought to live. Let's look at five competing suppositions and their implications.

Supposition 1: The origin of the universe was a random event, and there is no God.

Supposition 2: The origin of the universe was a random event; God exists but he is not involved in overseeing the universe.

Supposition 3: The origin of the universe was a random event; God exists and is actively involved in overseeing the universe.

Supposition 4: God created the universe, but he is not involved in
                overseeing it.
Supposition 5: God created the universe and is actively involved in
                overseeing it.

SUPPOSITION 1: RANDOM UNIVERSE, NO GOD

If the universe originated as a random event and there is no God, then our
present life is all that we have. The Bible would be irrelevant. Death would
be final. There would be no heaven or hell and no eternal rewards or punishments for the way people choose to live. There would be no moral absolutes
and no authoritative reasons for observing moral restraints. There would
be no higher power to call upon for help when we need it. If supposition 1
were true, everyone would be free to live in whatever way they choose, and
there would be no eternal consequences. Some people might choose lives of
accomplishment and service, finding fulfillment and a legacy in contributing
to the good of others. Some might choose lives of self-absorption and self-in-
dulgence. Other people might choose to drift through life a day at a time.

SUPPOSITION 2: RANDOM UNIVERSE, IMPERSONAL GOD

If the universe originated as a random event but God exists, then he
would not be the God that the Bible describes. Furthermore, he would not
be trustworthy, since he declared through Isaiah that it was he who created
the universe and everything in it.

> It is I who made the earth, and created man upon it. I stretched out the
> heavens with My hands and I ordained all their host [Isaiah 45:12].

Similarly, the Bible would not be trustworthy because the Book of
Jeremiah says of God,

> It is He who made the earth by His power, who established the world
> by His wisdom; and by His understanding He has stretched out the
> heavens [Jeremiah 10:12].

If those verses were not true, how could we be sure what else to believe
in the Bible? Is there eternal life? Do heaven and hell exist? Is salvation
possible? Perhaps, but perhaps not. If supposition 2 were true, it would be

futile to pray and seek God's help because he would not be involved in overseeing the universe. If this supposition were true, our best strategy would be to try to lead a life that was good enough and hope for the best.

Supposition 3: Random Universe, Personal God

This supposition has the same implications about God and the Bible as supposition 2, except that we could pray and hope for an answer because of God being involved in overseeing the universe. Our best strategy would still be to try to lead a life that was good enough and hope for the best.

Supposition 4: Created Universe, Impersonal God

This supposition also casts doubt upon the trustworthiness of the Bible. In this case it is because the Bible portrays God as being involved in overseeing the universe in general and the earth and mankind in particular, which this supposition rejects. If we subscribe to this supposition, it would be futile to pray and seek God's help. Our best strategy would still be to try to lead a life that was good enough and hope for the best.

Supposition 5: Created Universe, Personal God

In this supposition, which is the one this book advocates, the universe was God's idea and he created it. It exists within his domain, and he is actively and personally involved in overseeing it. We can trust God and we can believe what the Bible says about him. There are moral absolutes with benefits for conforming to them and consequences for violating them. Having a relationship with God is important. The way we treat people is also important. We do not cease to exist when we die. Heaven and hell are real, and there will be eternal rewards and punishments for the way we choose to live. We have the possibility of one day being reunited with friends and loved ones who have passed away. When we die physically, we will live forever with God, provided that we have previously met his conditions for acceptance into heaven. Trying to live a life that is good enough and hoping for the best is very risky. The strategy that makes the most sense is to find out what God has to say and then, to the best of our ability, conform to it.

Many people mentally agree with supposition 5 but choose a less-than-optimal approach. They read or hear about what God has said. Then they pick and choose which of his commandments and instructions to obey and which to ignore. That is not a well-thought-out plan. Even one mistake or miscalculation could result in disastrous unintended consequences. Remember what happened to Adam and Eve.

1-5

THE PHYSICAL UNIVERSE

Astrophysicists and astronomers have recently made a number of remarkable discoveries. Using powerful earth-based and space-based telescopes operating at radio, microwave, infrared, visible, ultraviolet, and x-ray frequencies, they have been able to observe features of the universe from the present day back almost to the moment of creation. Those observations help explain some of the events and processes that occurred during the development of the physical universe. Examples of recent scientific discoveries include stars being created from coalescing hydrogen gas, black holes and the way galaxies form and rotate around them, other stars with planets revolving around them, and the process of planets being formed from the residue of supernovas. And there are many mysteries still to be solved. An important one is the identity and characteristics of so-called dark energy and dark matter.

Scientists have discovered that there is nothing static about the universe. It is expanding, everything in it is in motion, and everything about it is in a state of constant change. God is not threatened by any of these scientific discoveries. In fact, I believe he is delighted that people have recently become intrigued to find out "how he did it."

There is a large segment of Christianity that feels threatened by scientific data about the universe and how it has developed. They fear that this information might somehow discredit what the Bible says and thereby damage or even destroy people's faith. Of course, erroneous ideas that some people hold about creation are threatened by scientific data. But we do not need to reject science in order to accept God's role in creation, and vice versa.

The Bible's primary focus is upon God's interactions with people. It has very little to say about the history of the physical universe or the processes by which the universe developed, other than to assure us that it was God who caused it all to happen.

The Lord by wisdom founded the earth,
By understanding He established the heavens [Proverbs 3:19].

By faith we understand that the worlds were prepared by the word of
God, so that what is seen was not made out of things which are visible
[Hebrews 11:3].

From a scientific viewpoint, Hebrews 11:3, which was written nearly
two thousand years ago, is a particularly interesting statement. We now
know that individual atoms comprise our material universe, and that they
are not visible to the unaided eye, nor are the subatomic particles which
comprise atoms visible to us.

The Bible says that Jesus played an important role in creation:

All things came into being through Him, and apart from Him nothing
came into being that has come into being [John 1:3].

The book of Proverbs has a remarkable passage that describes what it
was like for Jesus to be with the Father during creation. When we read that
passage, we get the impression that it was an absolutely delightful time for
him and the Father.

When He established the heavens, I was there,
When He inscribed a circle on the face of the deep,
When He made firm the skies above,
When the springs of the deep became fixed,
When He set for the sea its boundary
So that the water would not transgress His command,
When He marked out the foundations of the earth;
Then I was beside Him, as a master workman;
And I was daily His delight, rejoicing always before Him,
Rejoicing in the world, His earth,
And having my delight in the sons of men
[Proverbs 8:27–31].

If we believe that account, then we must accept that the heavens, and
especially the earth, did not come about through a series of random,
unguided occurrences. Their development was guided by God himself in
very intentional ways.

1-6

THE SPIRITUAL REALM

In addition to the physical universe, there is a spiritual realm that is invisible to us. This domain is the dwelling place of God and his angels, as well as Satan and his demons. In his epistles, Paul refers to the "heavenly places" and to "angels" and "principalities" dwelling there.

> Blessed be the God and Father of our Lord Jesus Christ, who has blessed us with every spiritual blessing in the heavenly places in Christ [Ephesians 1:3].

> Which he brought about in Christ, when He raised Him from the dead and seated Him at His right hand in the heavenly places, far above all rule and authority and power and dominion, and every name that is named, not only in this age but also in the one to come [Ephesians 1:20–21].

> For I am convinced that neither death, nor life, nor angels, nor principalities, nor things present, nor things to come, nor powers, nor height, nor depth, nor any other created thing, will be able to separate us from the love of God, which is in Christ Jesus our Lord [Romans 8:38–39].

Neither our physical senses nor our scientific instruments are able to detect the spiritual realm. Therefore neither we nor science can either prove or disprove its existence. We must accept by faith that what the Bible says is true.

The Bible discloses very little about the creation of the spiritual realm and its inhabitants beyond assuring us that it was God who created them.

> By the word of the Lord the heavens were made,
> And by the breath of his mouth all their host [Psalm 33:6].

> For by Him all things were created, both in the heavens and on earth, visible and invisible, whether thrones or dominions or rulers or authorities—all things have been created through Him and for Him [Colossians 1:16].

1-7

THE REBELLION AND
FALL OF SATAN

A tragic event occurred long ago in the spiritual realm: Satan's rebellion against God and God's kingdom. Scripture passages in Ezekiel 28, Isaiah 14, and Revelation 12 provide us with some insights into what happened. The passage in Ezekiel tells the story of the "king of Tyre," who was an earthly king but also a metaphor for Satan. Ezekiel initially describes Satan (as the king of Tyre) as perfect, wise, beautiful, and splendidly adorned. He was morally upright and had an important role in God's kingdom along with heavenly access and privileges. But then he sinned by rebelling against God. Ezekiel wrote about some of Satan's thoughts and actions that preceded his rebellion.

> Your heart was lifted up because of your beauty; you corrupted your wisdom by reason of your splendor [Ezekiel 28:17a].

> By the multitude of your iniquities, in the unrighteousness of your trade you profaned your sanctuaries [Ezekiel 28:18a].

Isaiah provided further details.

> But you said in your heart, "I will ascend to heaven; I will raise my throne above the stars of God, and I will sit on the mount of assembly in the recesses of the north. I will ascend above the heights of the clouds; I will make myself like the Most High" [Isaiah 14:13–14].

Satan, who is now the devil, deceived himself into believing that he could overthrow God and seize control of God's kingdom. He failed and his eventual punishment will be eternal imprisonment.

> Nevertheless you will be thrust down to Sheol, to the recesses of the pit [Isaiah 14:15].

Satan was not alone in his rebellion. Verses in Revelation 12 imply that a third of the angels joined that armed rebellion and were likewise expelled from heaven.

Then another sign appeared in heaven: and behold, a great red dragon
having seven heads and ten horns, and on his heads were seven diadems.
And his tail swept away a third of the stars of heaven and threw them to
the earth [Revelation 12:3–4a].

And there was war in heaven, Michael and his angels waging war with
the dragon. The dragon and his angels waged war, and they were not
strong enough, and there was no longer a place found for them in
heaven. And the great dragon was thrown down, the serpent of old
who is called the devil and Satan, who deceives the whole world; he was
thrown down to the earth, and his angels were thrown down with him
[Revelation 12:7–9].

Not only were there consequences for Satan and those angels who
followed him, there were consequences for Adam and Eve and repercus-
sions for us today. We all suffer as a result of Satan's rebellion and fall.

Put on the full armor of God, so that you will be able to stand firm
against the schemes of the devil. For our struggle is not against flesh
and blood, but against the rulers, against the powers, against the world
forces of this darkness, against the spiritual forces of wickedness in the
heavenly places [Ephesians 6:11–12].

Be of sober spirit, be on the alert. Your adversary, the devil, prowls around
like a roaring lion, seeking someone to devour. But resist him, firm in
your faith, knowing that the same experiences of suffering are being
accomplished by your brethren who are in the world [1 Peter 5:8–9].

1-8

ADAM AND EVE

A new era of the kingdom of God on the earth began when God created
Adam, planted the Garden of Eden in what today is Iraq, and placed
Adam there to cultivate, tend, and enjoy it (Genesis 2:7–15). God created
Eve to be Adam's wife and partner (Genesis 2:20–25). Those who believe that
Adam and Eve could not possibly have been special creations have a very
limited perception of the greatness and power of Almighty God. Whether or
not there were other people living on the earth at that time does not invalidate

the Genesis account. In the same way that mighty angels with flaming swords later prevented Adam and Eve from re-entering the garden (Genesis 3:24), angels could easily have kept anyone else from entering Eden while Adam and Eve were living there.

Let's consider the Genesis account as the report of an experiment conducted by God. The question being investigated was this: would perfectly created human beings, isolated in an ideal environment and living in a state of total innocence, appreciate what they had and live in obedience to God?

> The Lord God commanded the man, saying, "From any tree of the garden you may eat freely; but from the tree of the knowledge of good and evil you shall not eat, for in the day that you eat from it you will surely die" [Genesis 2:16–17].

The test was a simple one: do not eat fruit from the tree of the knowledge of good and evil. Evaluating their obedience was totally objective: did they eat any of the fruit? The penalty for disobedience was severe: it would mean death, which would include forfeiting everything they had. It seems like a no-brainer for Adam and Eve to tend the garden, enjoy a rich and full life together, and refrain from that one prohibition. So why did it not happen that way?

Because they were living in an earthly paradise, everything went extraordinarily well for them in the beginning. Since there were no physical dangers, perhaps they grew complacent, maybe even bored. God often visited them, but there were no other visitors. Then one day Satan showed up, disguised as a serpent (Genesis 3:1). That verse makes me wonder if conversations with animals were normal in the Garden of Eden. Satan was on a clandestine mission, a personal vendetta against God. His aim was to entice Adam and Eve into violating the one prohibition God had given them. Satan began gaining their confidence by demonstrating his knowledge of that prohibition.

> Now the serpent was more crafty than any beast of the field which the Lord God had made. And he said to the woman, "Indeed, has God said, 'You shall not eat from any tree of the garden'?" The woman said to the serpent, "From the fruit of the trees of the garden we may eat; but from the fruit of the tree which is in the middle of the garden, God has said, 'You shall not eat from it or touch it, or you will die'" [Genesis 3:1–3].

Notice that Eve added to what God had said. God told them "Do not eat the fruit;" he did not forbid their touching it.

Satan continued to represent himself as all-knowing, all-wise, and concerned only with what was best for them. Adam and Eve seemed to be unusually naïve. Of course, since God had been their only visitor, they had never heard either a lie or a partial truth. They accepted at face value everything that this stranger was telling them.

Next, Satan began to plant doubts about God's innate goodness. He said that God had lied to them: there would be no punishment. He implied that God was withholding something of great value from them, something that they deserved to have.

> The serpent said to the woman, "You surely will not die! For God knows that in the day you eat from it your eyes will be opened, and you will be like God, knowing good and evil" [Genesis 3:4–5].

Eve believed Satan's lie that God is not all-good and that he withholds good things from us. She was also intrigued by the idea of becoming equal with God. She didn't know that Satan had already proved that such a thing is not possible, and that trying to achieve it is disastrous.

> When the woman saw that the tree was good for food, and that it was a delight to the eyes, and that the tree was desirable to make one wise, she took from its fruit and ate [Genesis 3:6a].

Eve yielded to the temptation. She picked a fruit, an especially risky action since she had said that touching it would kill her. When she did not die immediately from touching it, she concluded that Satan was telling the truth and that God was not. She ate some of the fruit and did not die. And she gave also to her husband with her, and he ate (Genesis 3:6b).

Notice that Eve was not alone when those events occurred. Genesis 3:6 says that Adam was with her. A key question is why didn't he restrain her? Why didn't he say, "There's no hurry to do this, Eve. The tree will still have fruit on it next week. We have been given conflicting accounts. If God is telling the truth, then what we're considering doing will bring total disaster upon us. We will forfeit everything that we have and are. We need to find out what the truth is! Let's discuss this with God before we perhaps make a very foolish and irreversible mistake." But instead, Adam gave silent assent to what Eve wanted to do and then participated by eating some of the fruit himself. Suddenly their innocence vanished. Too late they realized that there were indeed consequences for their disobedience, as God had said there would be.

> Then the eyes of both of them were opened, and they knew that they were naked; and they sewed fig leaves together and made themselves loin coverings [Genesis 3:7].

Later that day God visited them. The remainder of Genesis 3 describes their conversation with him and his pronouncement of punishment. God affirmed that they would indeed die, although not immediately.

> By the sweat of your face you will eat bread, till you return to the ground, because from it you were taken; for you are dust, and to dust you shall return [Genesis 3:19].

> So all the days that Adam lived were nine hundred and thirty years, and he died [Genesis 5:5].

Human nature has not changed. First John 2:16 lists the same three categories of temptation that Satan used so successfully against Eve: the lust of the flesh (desiring pleasures), the lust of the eye (desiring possessions), and the boastful pride of life (desiring power and influence). During Jesus' wilderness temptations as described in Luke 4:1–13, Satan tried those same three types of enticements. Jesus successfully resisted Satan's temptations.

Let's revisit the original question: would perfectly created human beings, isolated in an ideal environment and living in a state of total innocence, appreciate what they had and live in obedience to God? Unfortunately the answer is no, they would not. For us, who are less perfect and live in an imperfect environment, it is even more difficult to remain obedient to God. But God did not abandon Adam and Eve when they disobeyed him, and he will not abandon us either. He provided atonement for their actions, restoring fellowship with himself. He has provided atonement for our actions as well, making a way to pardon us and restore fellowship with him. I'll say more about this later.

1-9

FROM ADAM TO ABRAHAM

If you do the math based upon the biblical genealogies in Genesis, you will calculate that Adam was created around 4000 B.C. During the two thousand years that followed, God did not institute any laws. People were allowed to and expected to live in accordance with their God-given conscience. According to Scripture, almost no one chose to have a close relationship with God during the period from Adam to Abraham. The Bible names only two: Enoch and Noah.

> Enoch lived sixty-five years, and became the father of Methuselah. Then Enoch walked with God three hundred years after he became the father of Methuselah, and he had other sons and daughters. So all the days of Enoch were three hundred and sixty-five years. Enoch walked with God; and he was not, for God took him [Genesis 5:21–24].

> But Noah found favor in the eyes of the Lord. These are the records of the generations of Noah. Noah was a righteous man, blameless in his time; Noah walked with God [Genesis 6:8–9].

Certainly there were many others to whom God reached out during that era, offering to establish a close relationship with them. I believe that he reached out to everyone who lived during that period. I believe that he still does. It is heartbreaking to think that throughout a two- thousand-year period, only Enoch and Noah responded to God in any significant way.

1-10

ABRAHAM

God's next recorded outreach was to Abram. God approached Abram and made him an offer. He proposed that Abram leave his country and his relatives and move to a yet-to-be-specified place. God promised him great blessings if he would.

> Now the Lord said to Abram, "Go forth from your country, and from your relatives and from your father's house, to the land which I will

show you; and I will make you a great nation, and I will bless you, and make your name great; and so you shall be a blessing; and I will bless those who bless you, and the one who curses you I will curse. And in you all the families of the earth will be blessed" [Genesis 12:1–3].

What an astonishing offer! It was a purposeful test of Abram's faith, his trust in God, and his willingness to obey God. How would he respond?

Have you ever wondered why God made that offer to Abram rather than to someone else? Certainly God had been evaluating people from earliest times. Abram may have been the first whose immediate descendants (even though as yet he had none) had the potential for following God and maintaining a close relationship with him. Adam's immediate descendants did not; neither did Enoch's nor Noah's.

However, Abram did exactly what God asked him to do, even though it meant great effort and faith on his part.

> So Abram went forth as the Lord had spoken to him; and Lot went with him. Now Abram was seventy-five years old when he departed from Haran. Abram took Sarai his wife and Lot his nephew, and all their possessions which they had accumulated, and the persons which they had acquired in Haran, and they set out for the land of Canaan; thus they came to the land of Canaan [Genesis 12:4–5].

Sometime after Abram arrived in Canaan, God appeared to him and promised the land to his descendants.

> The Lord appeared to Abram and said, "To your descendants I will give this land." So he built an altar there to the Lord who had appeared to him [Genesis 12:7].

Later God reiterated his promise.

> The Lord said to Abram, after Lot had separated from him, "Now lift up your eyes and look from the place where you are, northward and southward and eastward and westward; for all the land which you see, I will give it to you and to your descendants forever. I will make your descendants as the dust of the earth, so that if anyone can number the dust of the earth, then your descendants can also be numbered. Arise, walk about the land through its length and breadth; for I will give it to you" [Genesis 13:14–17].

God's promises of future blessings for Abram's descendants must have felt empty to Abram, and he reminded God that he had no descendants.

> After these things the word of the Lord came to Abram in a vision, saying, "Do not fear, Abram, I am a shield to you; your reward shall be very great." Abram said, "O Lord God, what will You give me, since I am childless, and the heir of my house is Eliezer of Damascus?" And Abram said, "Since You have given no offspring to me, one born in my house is my heir" [Genesis 15:1–3].

God promised Abram that he would indeed have descendants.

> Then behold, the word of the Lord came to him, saying, "This man will not be your heir; but one who will come forth from your own body, he shall be your heir" [Genesis 15:4].

God repeated his promise of Genesis 13:16 that Abram would have an uncountable number of descendants.

> And He took him outside and said, "Now look toward the heavens, and count the stars, if you are able to count them." And He said to him, "So shall your descendants be" [Genesis 15:5].

The next verse is the key to understanding Abram's relationship with God. And it conveys one of the fundamental concepts for successful living in God's kingdom.

> Then he believed in the Lord; and He [the Lord] reckoned it to him as righteousness [Genesis 15:6].

Even though what God had promised seemed utterly impossible, Abram believed that God could and would do what he had said. Because Abram believed God, God imputed righteousness to him. That is, God chose to consider Abram to be someone who had never sinned and had no tendency to sin. Abram's faith and obedience was also used as an example in the New Testament. Throughout Romans 4 Paul continually referred to Abraham's faith in believing God's promises. Hebrews 11:8–10 also referred to Abraham's faith in obeying God.

Abram's story gives us three fundamental concepts for successful living in the kingdom of God. The first two are our responsibility; the third is God's.

1)   Do what God tells us to do (Genesis 12:1,4–5).
2)   Believe that God will do what he has promised to do (Genesis 12:2–3,7; 13:14–17; 15:1,4–6).
3)   Then God will pour out his promised blessings upon us.

Let's revisit the account of Adam and Eve in the light of those three concepts. They were living in Eden, a paradise on earth. They were experiencing God's blessings of life, health, safety, joy, and abundance. But subsequent events showed that they did not believe God when he said that they would die if they ate the forbidden fruit. Because of their unbelief, they violated the one prohibition that God had given them. The immediate result of their disobedience was that God withdrew his best blessings, expelled them from Eden, and ended the carefree life they were enjoying. He later fulfilled his promise that they would die.

1-11

FROM ABRAHAM TO MOSES

In Genesis 12:2 God promised Abram that his descendants would become a great nation. Their being transformed into a nation was the next step in God's expansion of his kingdom on the earth.

The Middle East was not a safe place to live during Abram's time. For example, the Egyptian Pharaoh seized Abram's wife Sarai for his harem (Genesis 12), and Lot and his family were taken captive by a marauding army (Genesis 14). The surrounding nations would never have left Abram's descendants alone long enough for them to develop into a nation. But God had a plan for protecting them until they became populous enough and strong enough to be self-sufficient and self-protecting. God's plan was to have them live in Egypt for a while, where they would be under the protection of one of that era's most powerful nations. God told Abram that his descendants would live in a foreign country and would be enslaved and oppressed there for four hundred years (Genesis 15:13–14). It would not be an easy time, but it was an important part of God's plan for them.

In Genesis 17, when Abram was 99 years old, God appeared to him again and re-confirmed his promise that Abram would be the father of many nations. He changed Abram's name, which meant "exalted father," to

Abraham, which means "father of a multitude." Abraham became the father of Isaac. God repeated his promise to Isaac in Genesis 26:24. Isaac became the father of Jacob and God confirmed his promise to Jacob in Genesis 35:11–12. Then God changed Jacob's name, which meant "one who unseats or displaces" (which he had done to his twin brother Esau), to Israel, which means "having power with God."

Abraham's great-grandson Joseph was sold into slavery in Egypt through the jealousy and treachery of his brothers (Genesis 37). However, God blessed Joseph there and gave him great favor with Pharaoh, who appointed him to be the number two ruler in Egypt (Genesis 39–41). Because of his powerful and influential position, Joseph was able to relocate his father, his brothers, and their families to Egypt. He arranged for them to live in the very best land under the protection of the government (Genesis 46–47).

Mutually experienced hardships can cause people to bond together. Today's military uses that technique as one facet of basic training. Having Abraham's descendants bond into a cohesive unit was one of God's purposes for their being enslaved and oppressed. Another purpose was to make them turn to him, the only possible deliverer from their oppressors. Still another purpose was to allow them to build up a longing for freedom so that they would accept God's terms and methods for bringing them out of Egypt.

1-12

MOSES

Through highly unusual circumstances, the infant Moses was rescued and adopted by Pharaoh's daughter. He likely grew up in the palace with princely privileges and the finest available education (Exodus 2:1–10). When he was forty years old, he decided to visit his people, the Israelites. He was enraged at the way he saw them being treated by their Egyptian taskmasters. He saved the life of an Israelite slave by killing the Egyptian who was savagely beating him. When he returned the following day, he discovered that the Israelites had no appreciation for what he had just done for them. They failed to recognize him as either their protector or their potential deliverer.

When Pharaoh learned of the murder of the taskmaster, he sought to kill Moses. Moses fled to Midian in northwest Arabia. The Midianites were descendants of Abraham and his second wife Keturah. Moses later married the daughter of Jethro, the priest of Midian, and they had two sons. He worked as a shepherd for his father-in-law, a humble role for a former prince of Egypt. While Moses was living there, the pharaoh who sought to kill him died. About that same time, the Israelites, suffering in slavery, began to petition God to help them, and God heard their prayers (Exodus 2:23–25).

1-13

MOSES IS CALLED BY GOD

When Moses was eighty years old, an event occurred that permanently changed his life. While he was pasturing the flock near Mount Sinai, God spoke to him from a burning bush, calling him to deliver Israel from Egyptian bondage. Once the Israelites were released, Moses was to lead them to Canaan, the land that God had promised to Abraham's descendants more than four hundred years before.

> The Lord said, "I have surely seen the affliction of My people who are in Egypt, and have given heed to their cry because of their taskmasters, for I am aware of their sufferings. So I have come down to deliver them from the power of the Egyptians, and to bring them up from that land to a good and spacious land, to a land flowing with milk and honey, to the place of the Canaanite and the Hittite and the Amorite and the Perizzite and the Hivite and the Jebusite. Now, behold, the cry of the sons of Israel has come to Me; furthermore, I have seen the oppression with which the Egyptians are oppressing them. Therefore, come now, and I will send you to Pharaoh, so that you may bring My people, the sons of Israel, out of Egypt" [Exodus 3:7–10].

A stunned Moses asked God to identify himself.

> God said to Moses, "I AM WHO I AM"; and He said, "Thus you shall say to the sons of Israel, 'I AM has sent me to you.'" God, furthermore, said to Moses, "Thus you shall say to the sons of Israel, 'The Lord, the God of your fathers, the God of Abraham, the God of Isaac, and the God of Jacob, has sent me to you.' This is My name forever, and this is My memorial-name to all generations" [Exodus 3:14–15].

God dispatched Moses' brother Aaron to join him at Mount Sinai. Together they traveled back to Egypt. There they met with the elders of Israel and presented God's plan.

> So the people believed; and when they heard that the Lord was concerned about the sons of Israel and that He had seen their affliction, then they bowed low and worshiped [Exodus 4:31].

Moses and Aaron's first meeting with Pharaoh went very badly.

> And afterward Moses and Aaron came and said to Pharaoh, "Thus says the Lord, the God of Israel, 'Let My people go that they may celebrate a feast to Me in the wilderness.'" But Pharaoh said, "Who is the Lord that I should obey His voice to let Israel go? I do not know the Lord, and besides, I will not let Israel go."
>
> Then they said, "The God of the Hebrews has met with us. Please, let us go a three days' journey into the wilderness that we may sacrifice to the Lord our God, otherwise He will fall upon us with pestilence or with the sword."
>
> But the king of Egypt said to them, "Moses and Aaron, why do you draw the people away from their work? Get back to your labors!" Again Pharaoh said, "Look, the people of the land are now many, and you would have them cease from their labors!"
>
> So the same day Pharaoh commanded the taskmasters over the people and their foremen, saying, "You are no longer to give the people straw to make brick as previously; let them go and gather straw for themselves. But the quota of bricks which they were making previously, you shall impose on them; you are not to reduce any of it. Because they are lazy, therefore they cry out, 'Let us go and sacrifice to our God.' Let the labor be heavier on the men, and let them work at it so that they will pay no attention to false words" [Exodus 5:1–9].

1-14

THE TEN PLAGUES

G od initiated a series of confrontations with Pharaoh. At the beginning of each, Moses and Aaron would announce the way God would next strike Egypt. Then God would do as he promised, eventually performing ten unprecedented miracles as described in Exodus 7–11:

1) The Nile was turned to blood.
2) There were hoards of frogs.
3) There were clouds of gnats.
4) There were swarms of insects.
5) There was a deadly disease that struck Egypt's livestock.
6) There was an outbreak of boils on the Egyptians and their livestock.
7) There were violent hailstorms accompanied by thunder and lightning.
8) There was a devastating locust attack.
9) Deep darkness covered the land.
10) Finally, there was the death of the firstborn of all the Egyptian people and their cattle.

Egypt was helpless before the power of Almighty God. Each plague either made the Egyptians extremely uncomfortable or harmed them or their livestock. Besides crushing Pharaoh's resolve, the plagues demonstrated that God was overwhelmingly superior to Egypt's supposed gods (Exodus 12:12).

Throughout the plagues, Moses and Aaron's demand was not for Pharaoh to release Israel, even though that was God's ultimate intention. Their demand was merely that Israel be allowed to journey into the wilderness and celebrate a feast to God (Exodus 5:1).

During the first nine plagues, the Israelites had no role or responsibility, and God sovereignly protected them and their livestock. The tenth plague was different. To be protected from that plague, each Israelite family had to believe what God said and do what he told them through Moses and Aaron. If they did not, their firstborn sons would also die along with those of the Egyptians. God required the Israelites to begin adhering to the three kingdom principles that he had established from the beginning:

1)   Do what he says to do.
2)   Believe that he will do what he has promised (Exodus 12:1–
     13, 22–23, 28).
3)   Then he will fulfill his promises.

It was only after the tenth plague—the deaths of the firstborn of the
Egyptians and their cattle—that Pharaoh relented. Moses assembled the
people and led them toward the Red Sea. This was not some arbitrary path,
for God himself was leading them by means of a pillar of cloud during the
day and a pillar of fire at night (Exodus 13:17–22). Their exodus from Egypt
was a defining event for Israel. Though they lacked organization, government, and territory, they were now a free and independent nation.

1-15

CROSSING THE RED SEA

G od next initiated a series of training exercises to teach his new nation to
trust him and to live according to his kingdom principles. The first exercise began soon after they left their homes in Egypt. While they were camping
peacefully beside the Red Sea, Pharaoh changed his mind and ordered his
army to bring them back (Exodus 14:5–10). When the Israelites discovered
what was about to happen, they became overwhelmed with fear (Exodus
14:11–12). They lacked military training and organization and possessed few
weapons. They were certainly no match for Pharaoh's chariots and armed
soldiers.

Moses addressed the people, urging them not to be afraid but to believe
that God would save them (Exodus 14:13–14). God instructed Moses to
raise his staff aloft (Exodus 14:15–18). When he obeyed, the Red Sea parted
and Israel crossed through it, walking between two walls of water. When
Pharaoh's army tried to follow, the waters came back together and the
soldiers all drowned (Exodus 14:21–30).

> When Israel saw the great power which the Lord had used against the
> Egyptians, the people feared the Lord, and they believed in the Lord
> and in His servant Moses [Exodus 14:31].

1-16

THE JOURNEY TO MOUNT SINAI

It was time for Israel's next test: to discover how they would respond when they ran short of water. Finding water is particularly important when traveling through a desert. There were around two million people along with their flocks and herds, so they needed a large amount of drinking water every day. During one three-day march, there was no water along the route. When they arrived at Marah, they found water but it was not drinkable (Exodus 15:22–23).

> So the people grumbled at Moses, saying, "What shall we drink?" [Exodus 15:24].

Moses had no solution, but he knew who did.

> Then he cried out to the Lord, and the Lord showed him a tree; he threw it into the waters, and the waters became sweet [Exodus 15:25].

There are no magic trees in the Sinai Desert that can transform water that is not drinkable into water that is. God performed a miracle when Moses did as God told him. God was once again showing Israel that they must turn to him when human help is inadequate.

They journeyed on to Elim, a place with trees, good pastureland, and an abundance of water. The Lord allowed them rest and relax there for several weeks (Exodus 15:27).

Then it was time to continue on toward Mount Sinai and to undergo another test: What would they do when their food supply dwindled? The result was not pretty. Their response was not, "Let's turn to the Lord, who has repeatedly helped us. He will surely provide food for us." Instead, they grumbled again.

> The whole congregation of the sons of Israel grumbled against Moses and Aaron in the wilderness. The sons of Israel said to them, "Would that we had died by the Lord's hand in the land of Egypt, when we sat by the pots of meat, when we ate bread to the full; for you have brought us out into this wilderness to kill this whole assembly with hunger" [Exodus 16:2–3].

Despite their grumbling, God already had a plan. He would provide them with manna.

> Then the Lord said to Moses, "Behold, I will rain bread from heaven for you; and the people shall go out and gather a day's portion every day, that I may test them, whether or not they will walk in My instruction" [Exodus 16:4].

Notice the word "test" in that verse. The daily manna was yet another of God's unprecedented miracles. Nothing like it had happened in the history of the world. God's provision of manna became a daily miracle that continued uninterrupted, six days a week, for forty years. God's provision of manna continued until the day Israel entered Canaan. This is how Moses described what happened:

> He humbled you and let you be hungry, and fed you with manna which you did not know, nor did your fathers know, that He might make you understand that man does not live by bread alone, but man lives by everything that proceeds out of the mouth of the Lord [Deuteronomy 8:3].

The point was that people need God, not just the things he can provide. Jesus quoted from that verse when Satan challenged him to satisfy his hunger by turning stones into bread (Luke 4:4). An important lesson is to look to God to meet our needs, as the Lord's Prayer expresses:

> Give us this day our daily bread [Matthew 6:11].

Exodus 17:1–7 records another test and another failure. Israel still had not learned to turn to God when they needed help. The Lord led them to Rephidim and there was no water there, so they grumbled against Moses. In fact, they became so hostile that Moses expected them to stone him. He cried out to God, who pointed Moses to a certain rock, telling him to strike it with his staff. When he did, water rushed forth. And it was not a mere trickle. There was water for the people and their flocks and herds for the entire time they camped there.

> He [Moses] named the place Massah [meaning test] and Meribah [meaning quarrel] because of the quarrel of the sons of Israel, and because they tested the Lord, saying, "Is the Lord among us, or not?" [Exodus 17:7].

That incident was a particularly serious one, never to be forgotten. Moses referred to it years later in Deuteronomy 6:16:

> You shall not put the Lord your God to the test, as you tested Him at Massah.

Jesus quoted from that verse in rejecting Satan's third temptation:

> And Jesus answered and said to him, "It is said, 'You shall not put the Lord your God to the test'" [Luke 4:12].

While they were camped at Rephidim, the Israelites were attacked by the Amelekites, distant relatives descended from Jacob's twin brother Esau. Joshua marshaled an army and defeated them. A lesson for us is that even when we are being led by God, we may experience attacks, sometimes even from relatives. But as we continue to walk with God, he will protect us from harm.

1-17

THE GRAND VISION

Israel traveled the final leg to Mount Sinai (Exodus 19:2). After setting up camp there, Moses climbed the mountain to meet with God. God gave Moses a message for the Israelites that began,

> You yourselves have seen what I did to the Egyptians, and how I bore you on eagles' wings, and brought you to Myself [Exodus 19:4].

He reminded them of the supernatural power he had employed to free them from Egypt. He referred to his fatherly care and his miraculous provisions during their journey, comparing himself to an eagle teaching its young to fly. Then he came to the focal point of the message: his grand vision for Israel.

> "Now then, if you will indeed obey My voice and keep My covenant, then you shall be My own possession among all the peoples, for all the earth is Mine; and you shall be to Me a kingdom of priests and a holy

nation." These are the words that you shall speak to the sons of Israel
[Exodus 19:5–6].

God's grand vision had three main elements. First, he wanted the
Israelites to be his own possession, his special treasure, unique among
people. Deuteronomy 7:6b also recorded that intention, as did Deuteronomy
14:2b and Deuteronomy 26:18.

Second, it was God's desire that the entire nation be a kingdom of
priests. Priests serve as mediators between God and people. They represent God to people and intercede with God for people. God wanted every
Israelite to have a priestly role. There were two aspects to that: 1) they were
to be priests to their families, and 2) they were to be priests to other nations
and people, representing God to them and interceding with God on their
behalf. This declaration predated God's appointing Aaron as Israel's high
priest. Aaron and his descendants would minister to God in the tabernacle
and serve as priests to the people of Israel. The people of Israel were to serve
as priests to the rest of the world.

Third, it was God's intention that Israel be a holy nation consisting of
people who lived according to the covenant that he was about to make with
them. In Leviticus 20:26 God said,

> Thus you are to be holy to me, for I the Lord am holy; and I have set you
> apart from the peoples to be mine.

Peter quoted from that verse:

> But like the Holy One who called you, be holy yourselves also in all
> your behavior; because it is written, "You shall be holy, for I am holy"
> [1 Peter 1:15–16].

But God's grand vision for Israel was conditional. He began by saying,
"Now then, if you will indeed obey my voice and keep my covenant, then..."
The terms of that covenant are expressed in the Ten Commandments. The
requirement to obey God's voice was essential so that he could instruct,
direct, and correct them by speaking to them through their leaders and
prophets. If the nation would listen and obey, it would enjoy God's blessings. Similarly, each individual had the obligation to listen and obey when
God spoke in order to enjoy God's blessings for himself and his family. God
wanted to bless them continually:

Oh that they had such a heart in them, that they would fear Me and keep all My commandments always, that it may be well with them and with their sons forever! [Deuteronomy 5:29].

1-18

THE TERMS OF THE COVENANT: THE TEN COMMANDMENTS

God's purpose in giving the Ten Commandments was to clarify and codify everyone's responsibilities for establishing and maintaining appropriate relationships with God and with other people. The first four commandments define people's responsibilities toward God, and the last six commandments define people's responsibilities toward each other.

1) He is to be our only God.
2) We are not to create worship aids such as paintings, statues, and symbols and then worship those objects.
3) We are to be respectful of and not misuse God's name, for his name represents who he is.
4) We are to set aside one day each week to rest from working and to worship God.
5) We are to honor and respect our parents.
6) We must not murder anyone.
7) We must not commit adultery.
8) We must not steal from anyone.
9) We must not lie about anyone.
10) We must not covet (earnestly desire) anything that belongs to someone else.

God's grand vision was for Israel to be a model nation, a nation united through communal worship of God and adherence to moral civil laws. He wanted them to respect the life, property, marriage, reputation, character, and lifestyle of everyone. They were to be fair and just not only to fellow Israelites but also to foreigners. They were to be a visible demonstration of life in the kingdom of God. Then their character and their actions would draw people to God.

1-19

FROM MOSES TO SOLOMON

G od's objective was that Israel be governed as a theocracy with God
himself as king. Unfortunately, the people would not cooperate. The
next four hundred years were a constant parade of Israel's willfulness and
wrong actions. For example,

- When God told Israel that the time had come to occupy
  Canaan, rather than obeying God, they became afraid and
  refused to enter the Promised Land. As punishment, God
  ordered them to remain in the wilderness for forty years,
  until that generation of unbelievers died.
- When the forty years had passed, Joshua led Israel into
  Canaan. To reassure them of his presence and support, God
  supernaturally intervened during the siege of Jericho. God
  commanded Israel to capture all of Canaan and to drive out
  or annihilate the inhabitants. Israel stopped far short. The
  presence of Canaanites among them became a never-ending
  problem. Israel was continually influenced by the lifestyles,
  false gods, and worship styles of the Canaanites.
- After Joshua's death, Israel refused to accept another
  God-appointed national leader. As a result, during the era
  of the judges they never became the blessed and unified
  nation that God intended. Instead, they degenerated govern-
  mentally into a loose association of weak tribes. Each new
  generation of Israelites would drift away from God. God
  would then allow one of the surrounding nations to conquer
  them. In time they would cry out to God to free them. God
  would raise up a leader who led them to military victory and
  freedom. That pattern continually repeated itself.

Israel's most devastating fault, though, was its continual disregard for the
first two kingdom principles: 1) do what God says to do, and 2) believe that
God would then do as he promised. Because they refused to do their part,
the third kingdom principle was not activated: God did not pour out his
blessings upon them. What a monumental tragedy that was for Israel and
for the rest of the world.

Eventually Israel petitioned God to give them an earthly king. God reluctantly acquiesced and sent the prophet Samuel to anoint Saul to be their first king. Not long after Saul began his reign, he violated the first kingdom principle of doing what God told him. God rejected him as king and sent Samuel to anoint David as Saul's successor.

David became an outstanding king. He loved God deeply, trusted him fully, and always sought to obey him. Because of that, God blessed David beyond anything he could have imagined. Israel reached its pinnacle of prosperity, territorial extent, and influence under David and his son Solomon.

When Solomon succeeded David as king, God made him and his descendants a magnificent promise:

> As for you, if you will walk before Me as your father David walked, in integrity of heart and uprightness, doing according to all that I have commanded you and will keep My statutes and My ordinances, then I will establish the throne of your kingdom over Israel forever, just as I promised to your father David, saying, "You shall not lack a man on the throne of Israel" [1 Kings 9:4–5].

But God also gave him a stern warning:

> But if you or your sons indeed turn away from following Me, and do not keep My commandments and My statutes which I have set before you, and go and serve other gods and worship them, then I will cut off Israel from the land which I have given them, and the house which I have consecrated for My name, I will cast out of My sight. So Israel will become a proverb and a byword among all peoples. And this house will become a heap of ruins; everyone who passes by will be astonished and hiss and say, "Why has the Lord done thus to this land and to this house?" And they will say, "Because they forsook the Lord their God, who brought their fathers out of the land of Egypt, and adopted other gods and worshiped them and served them, therefore the Lord has brought all this adversity on them" [1 Kings 9:6–9].

1-20

FROM SOLOMON TO THE END OF THE OLD TESTAMENT

U pon Solomon's death, his son Rehoboam became king. He was not of the caliber of David or Solomon. Early in his reign the nation split. The tribes of Benjamin and Judah remained under him and took the name Judah. The other tribes took the name Israel. Jeroboam, a man not from David's lineage, became their king. To discourage Israel from reuniting with Judah, Jeroboam built Shechem as their capitol. He set up a new place of worship with two golden calves as their gods, in direct violation of God's first two commandments. From that time on, Judah and Israel were bitter enemies.

The next several hundred years witnessed the continual decline of Israel. Judah underwent a similar decline, interrupted by an occasional upturn when a good king came to the throne. During that entire period, God sent prophet after prophet to both of those nations with calls to repent, return to him, and live upright lives. As the time of each nation's destruction drew near, God sent still more prophets with urgent warnings. God's calls for repentance demanded appropriate responses by each person. Had a sufficient number of them so responded, Judah and Israel would have been spared. But neither the leaders nor the people would repent. Each nation was conquered: Israel by Assyria and Judah by Babylon.

Most of the inhabitants who survived were deported. Israel disappeared as a nation, intermarrying with and being absorbed into Assyria. Those who eventually migrated back to Canaan became the Samaritans of New Testament times. The small number of Judah's population who survived were the forefathers of the Jews. Most of the Jews were later dispersed throughout other nations of the world. Never again did a Jewish king reign over the land that had once been ruled by David and Solomon. With Israel and Judah eliminated as nations, the kingdom of God on the earth became essentially dormant until the arrival of Jesus.

1-21
SUMMARY

This chapter has provided a concise history of God's kingdom up to the coming of Jesus. God's kingdom is an eternal kingdom, with no beginning or end. It existed before God created the universe. The Bible says that God is personally involved in overseeing his kingdom on earth and the people in it.

God initiated his kingdom on earth through people, beginning with Adam and Eve. That didn't work out. Neither did any unrecorded attempts for the next two thousand years. God re-instituted his kingdom on earth through Abraham. It advanced through Abraham's family and their descendants, who became the nation of Israel. Israel, the nation that was supposed to live by the three kingdom principles, was initially governed as a theocracy. That government form did not survive past the time of Moses and Joshua. There followed the four-hundred-year period of the judges during which there was no continuing line of national leaders. After that Israel was ruled by kings. Other than during the reign of David and of Solomon, that didn't work out either. The people would not follow God consistently and therefore never enjoyed the full blessings of living in God's kingdom on earth.

Section 2

WHAT IS GOD LIKE?

2-1

INTRODUCTION

The kingdom of God is a manifestation of what God is like and how he behaves toward us. What is God really like and how does he behave toward us? As we investigate those questions, it is important to draw our information from the most reliable sources. We will start by thinking about the characteristics we would like God to have if we could specify them. Then we will look in some depth at what the Bible says about him. The two descriptions turn out to be surprisingly similar.

2-2

DIVERGENT IDEAS ABOUT GOD

Three people were describing God. The first began, "The Bible says..." The second started with, "Our church teaches..." The third said, "Well, it seems to me..." Unfortunately, too many people fall into the category of having an "it seems to me" God.

Paul Froese and Christopher Bader devised a questionnaire to aid them in investigating what Americans think God is like. Their resulting book, *America's Four Gods,* reported that there are many areas of concurrence. For instance, nearly everyone in America agrees that "God is love." But there are two topics on which they found wide ranges of beliefs. The first was how judgmental God is. People's beliefs covered the spectrum from believing that he is completely non-judgmental to believing that he is highly judgmental. The other main area of disagreement concerns the extent to which God is involved in people's lives. Based upon the beliefs about those two topics, the authors defined four points of view people have about God.

1)   The *distant* God, who is uninvolved with us and is non-judgmental of our thoughts and actions
2)   The *critical* God, who is uninvolved with us but is highly judgmental about what we think and do

3) The *benevolent* God, who is very much involved with us and is non-judgmental

4) The *authoritative* God, who is very much involved with us and is highly judgmental

Although we all have a set of beliefs about God's involvement or judgment in our lives, we cannot necessarily offer concrete proof for what we believe. In other words, none of us can know for sure exactly how God has been involved in our lives. Similarly we cannot be certain about how judgmental he is toward us. The bottom line is that compared to the reality of who God is, all of us are going to have some erroneous ideas.

America's Four Gods discusses a number of ways in which we are affected by our beliefs about God. They include our personal identity, self-esteem, morals, and political views. They include our attitudes toward other people as well as toward money, science, religion, and evil. What we believe about God influences the way we think, act, and live. It impacts our lifestyles, relationships, and many of our decisions.

There are many reasons for us to have different perceptions about God. Each of us is a unique, multifaceted person. Our life stories are distinctive, as are the factors that have shaped our beliefs about God.

There are three primary sources from which we draw information about what he is like. The first is the things we read, hear, and are taught. The second is the things that happen to us or to someone we know. The third is what God has revealed about himself through creation, his acts in the world, and the Bible. Our interpretations of these information sources often conflict with one another. Our challenge is to distinguish the information that is true from that which may be only partially true or is completely untrue.

We all have views of what God is like, but it is likely that he is not entirely as we suppose him to be. Because what we believe about him has a significant impact on the way we think and live, it is important that we move from believing in an "it-seems-to-me god" to finding out who he truly is and what he is actually like. Before we go there, let's first reflect on the characteristics most of us want God to have.

2-3

WHAT SORT OF GOD DO WE WANT?

Have you ever taken the time to think about what characteristics you would want God to have? Let's make a list now. It is probably easier to think of ways that we do not want a god to behave, so we will start there.

1)   We do not want a god who lies.
2)   We do not want a god who is untrustworthy.
3)   We do not want a god who is unfaithful.
4)   We do not want a god who dislikes us.
5)   We do not want a god who is harsh or mean.
6)   We do not want a god who is stingy.
7)   We do not want a god who is aloof, unapproachable, unavailable, or inattentive to us, for how could we then get his help when we need it?
8)   We do not want a god who is overly demanding.
9)   We do not want a god who is capricious, for then we would never be sure what behavior is or is not acceptable to him at the moment.
10)   We do not want a god who behaves badly.
11)   We do not want a god who is less intelligent than we are.
12)   We do not want a god who is unaware of what is happening in the world, and especially to us.
13)   We do not want a god who is impatient with us or who is intolerant of our shortcomings, weaknesses, and mistakes.
14)   We do not want a god who is unjust.
15)   We do not want a god who is vengeful.
16)   We do not want a god who is weak.
17)   We do not want a god who is unimpressive.
18)   We do not want a god who is mediocre or inferior.
19)   We do not want a god who can get sick or die.
20)   We do not want a god who is flawed or imperfect.

Next let's restate each of these items as a positive quality that we would like God to have.

1)   We want a god who is truthful.

2) We want a god who is trustworthy.
3) We want a god who is faithful.
4) We want a god who likes us.
5) We want a god who is kind and gracious.
6) We want a god who is generous.
7) We want a god who is approachable and available to us.
8) We want a god whose demands are reasonable.
9) We want a god who is consistent and unchanging.
10) We want a god who behaves righteously.
11) We want a god who is highly intelligent.
12) We want a god who is aware of what is happening in the world, especially around us and to us.
13) We want a god who is patient with us and is tolerant of our shortcomings, weaknesses, and mistakes.
14) We want a god who is just.
15) We want a god who is merciful.
16) We want a god who is strong and powerful.
17) We want a god who is impressive.
18) We want a god who is superior.
19) We want a god who cannot get sick or die.
20) We want a god who has no flaws or imperfections.

We have listed a set of the positive qualities we would like God to have. As we browse through our list, it looks as if we want a god who has the characteristics of an ideal, loving, caring, providing, and protecting parent, only much better.

Notice that every item in our list leaves room for improvement. Let's restate each quality, this time asking for the ultimate for each one.

1) We want a god who is absolutely truthful.
2) We want a god who is completely trustworthy.
3) We want a god who is unfailingly faithful.
4) We want a god who loves us very much.
5) We want a god who is always kind and gracious.
6) We want a god who is exceedingly generous.
7) We want a god who is readily approachable and always available to us.
8) We want a god who is minimally demanding.
9) We want a god who is always consistent, who never changes.

10) We want a god who always behaves righteously.
11) We want a god with unlimited knowledge, wisdom, and intelligence.
12) We want a god who is fully aware of and attentive to everything that is happening, especially around us and to us.
13) We want a god who completely understands us and is exceedingly patient with our shortcomings, weaknesses, and mistakes.
14) We want a god who is totally just.
15) We want a god who is unfailingly merciful.
16) We want a god who is almighty, who has unlimited power.
17) We want a god who is majestic beyond imagination.
18) We want a god who is superior to every other being in the universe.
19) We want a god who is eternal.
20) We want a god who is perfect in every way.

Except that we avoided using religious terminology, this sounds like a description of the God of the Bible, doesn't it? Who would have foreseen that? Let's now take an in-depth look at how the Bible describes God.

2-4

GOD IS HOLY

One notable absence from our wish list is for a god who is holy—indeed, who is the ultimate in holiness. The concept of God being holy is off-putting to many people. One reason may be that when we try to visualize God's holiness, we tend to picture him sitting on an elevated throne in heaven as Isaiah 6 describes. In Isaiah's vision, God seemed to be aloof, unwelcoming, unapproachable, demanding, and dwelling in a sterile environment guarded by bizarre creatures. As a result we may recoil when we read in the Bible that God is holy. Another reason the idea of a holy God may be off-putting is that holiness seems to be unattainable by our own efforts. And it is. But we do not want a god who is unholy, do we? Or a god who is somewhat holy but has room for improvement? Of course not!

Let's see if we can understand what the Bible means when it says that God is holy. The most common dictionary definition of *holy* is "set apart." That definition applies most appropriately to objects that have been consecrated for religious purposes, such as altars, crosses, and church buildings. However, "set apart" hardly seems an adequate definition of holy when it refers to God. Surely God's holiness means much more than that. And it does.

There are two illustrations in Scripture that especially shed light on God's holiness. In Isaiah 6:3 the seraphim proclaimed, "Holy, holy, holy is the Lord of hosts..." Revelation 4:8 says that the seraphim declare continually day and night, without ceasing, "Holy, holy, holy is the Lord God, the Almighty..." From these verses it is evident that God's holiness is something truly remarkable and immensely important. Otherwise, the seraphim mentioning it a few times would have been sufficient. But Revelation says that they proclaim it continually day and night.

That God is holy—in fact, the ultimate in holiness—is unique to him and is perhaps his most exceptional characteristic. How might we describe what God being holy means? Because of the unity of the Father, the Son, and the Holy Spirit, our description must apply to all three of them. I propose the following:

> God is of the highest possible excellence. He is transcendently pure, moral, and virtuous. He is completely sinless, being forever free of any wrongdoing, impurity, or defilement. He is absolutely faultless and blameless.

> God is high above and superior to everything else that exists. He is of a higher order, of a higher nature, and has a higher value than anything in creation, including the angels and the other heavenly beings. He is superior to them in every good quality. He is God Most High.

> God is the epitome of perfection. He is perfect in love, absolutely truthful, perfect in integrity, perfect in goodness and mercy, perfect in righteousness and justice, and completely honorable. He is exalted, worthy of total devotion, worthy of all honor and respect, worthy of all praise, and worthy of all worship.

The following verses speak about God's holiness:

Who is like You among the gods, O Lord? Who is like You, majestic in holiness, awesome in praises, working wonders? [Exodus 15:11].

For thus says the high and exalted One who lives forever, whose name is Holy, "I dwell on a high and holy place, and also with the contrite and lowly of spirit in order to revive the spirit of the lowly and to revive the heart of the contrite" [Isaiah 57:15].

The author of Psalm 99 expressed his admiration of God's holiness by writing,

Exalt the Lord our God
And worship at His holy hill,
For holy is the Lord our God [Psalm 99:9].

When our son Jake was six or seven years old, he loved to play in a swampy area near our house. When he came home covered in mud and plant matter, he was still our son and we still loved him. However, in that condition he was not fit to come into our clean house. We had a laundry sink in the garage. My wife Brenda washed him in it, dried him off, and then he could come inside.

We are God's beloved children, but we often need to be cleaned up. God is holy, and there is a day coming when he will make us holy as well. When that happens, we will be freed from our sinful nature and will be transformed into his likeness.

Yet He has now reconciled you in His fleshly body through death, in order to present you before Him holy and blameless and beyond reproach [Colossians 1:22].

Beloved, now we are children of God, and it has not appeared as yet what we will be. We know that when He appears, we will be like Him, because we will see Him just as He is [1 John 3:2].

Now let's walk through our list of the ways we want God to be and see how closely those characteristics match what God reveals about himself in the Bible. Since our list is lengthy, I have subdivided it into groups of related characteristics. I retained the item numbers as a convenient reference.

2-5

TRUTHFUL, TRUSTWORTHY, AND FAITHFUL

1) GOD IS TRUTHFUL

The first item in our original list was that we do not want a god who lies, one who gives us false information with the intention of misleading or deceiving us. If we wanted to serve such a liar, we could turn to Satan, about whom Jesus said,

> He was a murderer from the beginning, and does not stand in the truth because there is no truth in him. Whenever he speaks a lie, he speaks from his own nature, for he is a liar and the father of lies [John 8:44b].

God never lies; he is always truthful.

> God is not a man, that He should lie, nor a son of man, that He should repent; has He said, and will He not do it? Or has He spoken, and will He not make it good? [Numbers 23:19].

When he described himself to Moses, God declared that he is more than just truthful: he abounds in truth.

> Then the Lord passed by in front of him [Moses] and proclaimed, "The Lord, the Lord God, compassionate and gracious, slow to anger, and abounding in lovingkindness and truth" [Exodus 34:6].

Jesus taught that God is true.

> Then Jesus cried out in the temple, teaching and saying, "You both know Me and know where I am from; and I have not come of Myself, but He who sent Me is true, whom you do not know" [John 7:28].

John also taught that God is true.

> And we know that the Son of God has come, and has given us understanding so that we may know Him who is true; and we are in

Him who is true, in His Son Jesus Christ. This is the true God and
eternal life [1 John 5:20].

Witnesses in courtrooms in the United States swear to "tell the truth, the
whole truth, and nothing but the truth." In the same way, God tells the truth
and nothing but the truth; however, there is some information he chooses
not to reveal to us. Some truth is known only to God, as Moses wrote,

The secret things belong to the Lord our God, but the things revealed
belong to us and to our sons forever, that we may observe all the words
of this law [Deuteronomy 29:29].

God is entirely truthful, and he chooses which truth to reveal to us for
our good. It is important for us to realize this fact because it enables us to
trust him. The second principle of living in the kingdom of God is to believe
that God will do what he says he will do. We can only do that if everything
he says is always the truth, which is why Scripture reassures us:

Now, O Lord God, You are God, and Your words are truth [2 Samuel
7:28a].

2) GOD IS TRUSTWORTHY

When we trust God, it means that we have confidence in him. It means
that we rely upon him, knowing that he will never fail us.

I will say to the Lord, "My refuge and my fortress,
My God, in whom I trust!" [Psalm 91:2].

Trust in the Lord with all your heart
And do not lean on your own understanding.
In all your ways acknowledge Him,
And He will make your paths straight [Proverbs 3:5–6].

Trust in the Lord forever, for in God the Lord, we have an everlasting
Rock [Isaiah 26:4].

We can trust God because he is trustworthy. One who is trustworthy is
honorable, upstanding, dependable, reliable, truthful, and steadfast. God is
all of those.

The Lord is my strength and my shield;
My heart trusts in Him, and I am helped;
Therefore my heart exults,
And with my song I shall thank Him [Psalm 28:7].

Commit your way to the Lord,
Trust also in Him, and He will do it [Psalm 37:5].

We can trust God with our families and our careers. We can trust him with our hopes and dreams. How wonderful that we have a God whom we can confidently trust with every aspect of our lives and our futures.

3) God Is Faithful

One who is faithful is reliable and dependable. The faithfulness of God is closely related to his truthfulness and his trustworthiness.

The Lord's lovingkindnesses indeed never cease,
For His compassions never fail.
They are new every morning;
Great is Your faithfulness [Lamentations 3:22–23].

God's faithfulness ensures he will fulfill his covenants with us and will keep his promises to us.

Know therefore that the Lord your God, He is God, the faithful God, who keeps His covenant and His lovingkindness to a thousandth generation with those who love Him and keep His commandments [Deuteronomy 7:9].

Let us hold fast the confession of our hope without wavering, for He who promised is faithful [Hebrews 10:23].

We say concerning a dependable person that he keeps his word. God keeps his word.

Then the Lord said to me, "You have seen well, for I am watching over My word to perform it" [Jeremiah 1:12].

"For I the Lord will speak, and whatever word I speak will be performed. It will no longer be delayed, for in your days, O rebellious house, I will speak the word and perform it," declares the Lord God [Ezekiel 12:25].

Knowing that God is faithful and keeps his word helps us live with hope and confidence.

2-6

THE UNITY OF HIS QUALITIES

These four qualities—that God is holy, truthful, trustworthy, and faithful—are not isolated character traits. They are interrelated, blending into and harmonizing with one another. Because God is holy, he must also be truthful, trustworthy, and faithful. God is faithful, so he is also trustworthy and truthful. Because he is each of these things, we can believe him, put our confidence in him, and rely upon him. We can trust him because what he does is an expression of who he is.

We will continue addressing God's qualities individually and in small groups because that enables us to learn more about him without the descriptions becoming overly complex. Even so, we should keep the unity of God's characteristics in mind, for he is a complete and perfect whole.

2-7

LOVING, KIND, COMPASSIONATE, AND GRACIOUS

4) GOD IS LOVE

Love can be defined as a deep, tender feeling of affection or caring. It is intangible: we cannot see or hear or touch or smell it. Even so, we can sense it from another person as well as from God. Someone's love for us is often evident in their countenance, especially in their eyes.

The authors of *America's Four Gods* established that nearly all Americans agree with the statement, "God is love." And he is. God has a deep, abiding love for each of us. He asserts his love again and again throughout the Bible. Jesus affirmed it in the familiar words of John 3:16: "For God so loved the world, that He gave His only begotten Son, that whoever believes in Him shall not perish, but have eternal life." Jesus died for us, not so that God would love us, but because God does love us so deeply! God's unbounded love for people was the motivation for Calvary. Paul wrote,

> But God, being rich in mercy, because of His great love with which He loved us, even when we were dead in our transgressions, made us alive together with Christ [by grace you have been saved], and raised us up with Him, and seated us with Him in the heavenly places in Christ Jesus, so that in the ages to come He might show the surpassing riches of His grace in kindness toward us in Christ Jesus [Ephesians 2:4–7].

Real love's focus is always on the person who is loved. It seeks the very best for him or her. First Corinthians 13:4–7 is a description of ideal love, the kind of love God has for us, the kind of love that we should aspire to have for God and for other people.

> Love is patient, love is kind and is not jealous; love does not brag and is not arrogant, does not act unbecomingly; it does not seek its own, is not provoked, does not take into account a wrong suffered, does not rejoice in unrighteousness, but rejoices with the truth; bears all things, believes all things, hopes all things, endures all things.

Another way to describe God's love is like the love of a perfect father. John wrote,

> See how great a love the Father has bestowed on us, that we would be called children of God; and such we are [1 John 3:1a].

God's love has no limits. It is so vast that without his help we can't even begin to grasp its scope. It was for that reason that Paul offered this prayer for us:

> That you, being rooted and grounded in love, may be able to comprehend with all the saints what is the breadth and length and height and depth, and to know the love of Christ which surpasses knowledge, that you may be filled up to all the fullness of God [Ephesians 3:17b–19].

In addition, God's love is so powerful that nothing can impede it.

For I am convinced that neither death, nor life, nor angels, nor principalities, nor things present, nor things to come, nor powers, nor height, nor depth, nor any other created thing, will be able to separate us from the love of God, which is in Christ Jesus our Lord [Romans 8:38–39].

5) GOD IS KIND, COMPASSIONATE, AND GRACIOUS

One day while Israel was camped at Mount Sinai, Moses asked God to show him his glory. The following day, God did.

The Lord descended in the cloud and stood there with him as he called upon the name of the Lord. Then the Lord passed by in front of him and proclaimed, "The Lord, the Lord God, compassionate and gracious, slow to anger, and abounding in lovingkindness and truth" [Exodus 34:5–6].

That verse recounts God, in his own words, telling Moses what he is like. God chose to remind Moses that he is compassionate, gracious, slow to anger, and full of lovingkindness and truth.

Kindness

To be kind is to be thoughtful, understanding, and considerate. First Corinthians 13:4b says kindness is one of the characteristics of love. God's most notable demonstration of his kindness was in providing salvation for us through Jesus Christ.

But God, being rich in mercy, because of His great love with which He loved us, even when we were dead in our transgressions, made us alive together with Christ [by grace you have been saved], and raised us up with Him, and seated us with Him in the heavenly places in Christ Jesus, so that in the ages to come He might show the surpassing riches of His grace in kindness toward us in Christ Jesus [Ephesians 2:4–7].

Compassion

Compassion is more than simply concern and tenderheartedness toward someone. It is characterized by a deep awareness of that person's suffering and an intense desire to relieve that suffering. God has compassion toward us.

Just as a father has compassion on his children,
So the Lord has compassion on those who fear Him [Psalm 103:13].

Gracious is the Lord, and righteous;
Yes, our God is compassionate [Psalm 116:5].

Therefore the Lord longs to be gracious to you, and therefore He waits
on high to have compassion on you [Isaiah 30:18a].

Lovingkindness

The Bible often uses the word "lovingkindness." God's lovingkindness refers to his compassion, graciousness, and kindness toward us, motivated by his love for us. In the words of the Ten Commandments, God described himself as "showing lovingkindness to thousands, to those who love me and keep my commandments" (Exodus 20:6). First Chronicles 16:34 urges us, "O give thanks to the Lord, for He is good; for His lovingkindness is everlasting." Psalm 100:5 says, "For the Lord is good; His lovingkindness is everlasting and His faithfulness to all generations."

Graciousness

Someone who is gracious is kind, considerate, courteous, and tactful. God is gracious.

Gracious is the Lord, and righteous;
Yes, our God is compassionate [Psalm 116:5].

The Lord is compassionate and gracious,
Slow to anger and abounding in lovingkindness [Psalm 103:8].

Because God desires to extend his graciousness to us, God instructed Aaron and the priests to regularly pronounce this blessing upon people:

The Lord bless you, and keep you;
The Lord make His face shine on you,
And be gracious to you;
The Lord lift up His countenance on you,
And give you peace [Numbers 6:24–26].

2-8

GOOD

6) God Is Generous and Benevolent

When we read in the Bible that God is good, we probably think of his being virtuous and morally perfect. He does indeed have those qualities, but the Bible is not usually referring to them when it says that God is good. It is referring to his generosity and his benevolence. It is referring to the good things that he does and has done.

> You are good and do good [Psalm 119:68a].

> The Lord is good to all [Psalm 145:9a].

The earth is a terrific example of his goodness.

> God saw all that He had made, and behold, it was very good [Genesis 1:31a].

Moses' father-in-law was amazed by God's benevolence. "Jethro rejoiced over all the goodness which the Lord had done to Israel, in delivering them from the hand of the Egyptians" (Exodus 18:9). Later Moses reminded Israel of God's benevolence toward them. "In the wilderness He fed you manna which your fathers did not know, that He might humble you and that He might test you, to do good for you in the end" (Deuteronomy 8:16). God continued his generosity and benevolence toward Israel by giving them Canaan.

> For the Lord your God is bringing you into a good land, a land of brooks of water, of fountains and springs, flowing forth in valleys and hills [Deuteronomy 8:7].

> They captured fortified cities and a fertile land. They took possession of houses full of every good thing, hewn cisterns, vineyards, olive groves, fruit trees in abundance. So they ate, were filled and grew fat, and reveled in Your great goodness [Nehemiah 9:25].

God was not just good to Israel in the distant past; he has been good to people throughout history. And he is good to us today.

> And we know that God causes all things to work together for good to those who love God, to those who are called according to His purpose [Romans 8:28].

> Surely goodness and lovingkindness will follow me all the days of my life, And I will dwell in the house of the Lord forever [Psalm 23:6].

2-9

APPROACHABLE

7) GOD IS ACCESSIBLE AND AVAILABLE

If we attempted to spend some time every day with the president of the United States—getting to know him better, discussing ideas with him, presenting requests to him on behalf of ourselves and others—we would soon realize there is absolutely no chance of our getting to do that. Contrast that with our access to God. It's incredible by comparison, for God is continually available to us in prayer. And the Bible encourages us to make use of that wonderful privilege.

> Be anxious for nothing, but in everything by prayer and supplication with thanksgiving let your requests be made known to God [Philippians 4:6].

Jesus provided us with a model by often spending time in prayer with God.

> In the early morning, while it was still dark, Jesus got up, left the house, and went away to a secluded place, and was praying there [Mark 1:35].

> After He had sent the crowds away, He went up on the mountain by Himself to pray; and when it was evening, He was there alone [Matthew 14:23].

Jesus taught guiding principles for how to pray effectively.

When you pray, you are not to be like the hypocrites; for they love to
stand and pray in the synagogues and on the street corners so that they
may be seen by men. Truly I say to you, they have their reward in full
But you, when you pray, go into your inner room, close your door and
pray to your Father who is in secret, and your Father who sees what is
done in secret will reward you. And when you are praying, do not use
meaningless repetition as the Gentiles do, for they suppose that they
will be heard for their many words. So do not be like them; for your
Father knows what you need before you ask Him. Pray, then, in this way:

Our Father who is in heaven,
Hallowed be Your name.
Your kingdom come.
Your will be done,
On earth as it is in heaven.
Give us this day our daily bread.
And forgive us our debts, as we also have forgiven our debtors.
And do not lead us into temptation, but deliver us from evil.
For Yours is the kingdom and the power and the glory forever. Amen
    [Matthew 6:5–13].

And all things you ask in prayer, believing, you will receive [Matthew
21:22].

At those times when we would like to pray about some specific need or
situation but aren't sure how, the Holy Spirit is available to help us.

In the same way the Spirit also helps our weakness; for we do not know
how to pray as we should, but the Spirit Himself intercedes for us with
groanings too deep for words [Romans 8:26].

2-10

REQUIREMENTS

8) GOD IS MINIMALLY DEMANDING

A disciple is someone who subscribes to the teachings of a master and
assists in spreading those teachings. We have a calling to be disciples of

Jesus Christ. Perhaps the most important aspect of that calling is to become more like Jesus.

> It is enough for the disciple that he become like his teacher [Matthew 10:25a].

Another important aspect of that calling is to listen to him and do as he tells us.

> For this is the love of God, that we keep His commandments; and His commandments are not burdensome [1 John 5:3].

> So Jesus was saying to those Jews who had believed Him, "If you continue in My word, then you are truly disciples of Mine" [John 8:31].

When God assigns us a task, he expects us to do it. That is the first kingdom principle. In Jesus' parable of the talents, each of the servants who did as their master asked was praised and rewarded. The one who did not was chastised and punished (Matthew 25:14–30).

As Jesus' disciples, we are to perform our assignments, not as if we were being bossed by an Egyptian slave driver, but as co-workers with Jesus.

> Take My yoke upon you and learn from Me, for I am gentle and humble in heart, and you will find rest for your souls. For My yoke is easy and My burden is light [Matthew 11:29–30].

God is not a demanding taskmaster. He does not work us to exhaustion but instead gives us rest whenever we need it. That was one of his purposes in giving the fourth commandment: that we, our employees, and our farm animals would have a day of rest every week.

Jesus said,

> Come to Me, all who are weary and heavy-laden, and I will give you rest [Matthew 11:28].

David wrote,

> He makes me lie down in green pastures;
> He leads me beside quiet waters.
> He restores my soul [Psalm 23:2–3a].

There is one more requirement that is important to mention. We must help others become Jesus' disciples.

> Go therefore and make disciples of all the nations, baptizing them in the name of the Father and the Son and the Holy Spirit [Matthew 28:19].

> My Father is glorified by this, that you bear much fruit, and so prove to be My disciples [John 15:8].

2-11

UNCHANGING

9) GOD IS CONSTANT

Living as we do in a world and a universe that are in continuous motion, we are accustomed to constant change. Stars are born, give forth light for millions or billions of years, and then die. Here on earth, mountains are thrust up and then slowly erode. Rivers change course. The seasons cycle. Day turns to night and back to day. Nonetheless, God remains the same.

> Of old You founded the earth,
> And the heavens are the work of Your hands.
> Even they will perish, but You endure;
> And all of them will wear out like a garment;
> Like clothing You will change them and they will be changed.
> But You are the same,
> And Your years will not come to an end [Psalm 102:25–27].

We need not fear that God might somehow be different now than he has always been, or that he might become different in the future. He is constant. He is consistent. There is no variableness with him.

> Every good thing given and every perfect gift is from above, coming down from the Father of lights, with whom there is no variation or shifting shadow [James 1:17].

We can be confident that he will always be exactly the same.

I AM WHO I AM [Exodus 3:14a].

For I, the Lord, do not change [Malachi 3:6a].

As an often-quoted verse says,

Jesus Christ is the same yesterday and today and forever [Hebrews 13:8].

2-12

VIRTUOUS

10) GOD IS RIGHTEOUS

Righteousness entails morality, integrity, ethics, honor, and justice. God is righteous.

The Rock! His work is perfect,
For all His ways are just;
A God of faithfulness and without injustice,
Righteous and upright is He [Deuteronomy 32:4].

He behaves honorably.

For the Lord our God is righteous with respect to all His deeds which He has done [Daniel 9:14b].

Great and marvelous are Your works,
O Lord God, the Almighty;
Righteous and true are Your ways,
King of the nations! [Revelation 15:3b].

His laws are virtuous and impartial.

Or what great nation is there that has statutes and judgments as righteous as this whole law which I am setting before you today? [Deuteronomy 4:8].

And his judgments are upright.

The judgments of the Lord are true; they are righteous altogether [Psalm 19:9b].

Righteous are You, O Lord,
And upright are Your judgments [Psalm 119:137].

2-13

WISE AND ATTENTIVE

11) GOD HAS KNOWLEDGE, UNDERSTANDING, AND WISDOM

Knowledge is familiarity with information. *Understanding* is comprehension and interpretation of that information and the way it fits with other information. *Wisdom* is the ability to apply knowledge and understanding in order to make good plans and decisions and to choose appropriate courses of action.

God has all knowledge, understanding, and wisdom. He is far beyond brilliant. First Samuel 2:3 says that he is a God of knowledge. Psalm 147:5 says that his understanding is infinite. Daniel 2:2 says that wisdom and power belong to him. God never has to say, "Gosh, I didn't know that," or, "I'm sorry, but I don't understand that," or, "That caught me by surprise. I don't know what to do about that."

> Oh, the depth of the riches both of the wisdom and knowledge of God! How unsearchable are His judgments and unfathomable His ways! [Romans 11:33].

God, who has all knowledge, understanding, and wisdom, shares them with us when we ask him.

> But if any of you lacks wisdom, let him ask of God, who gives to all generously and without reproach, and it will be given to him [James 1:5].

> For the Lord gives wisdom;
> From His mouth come knowledge and understanding [Proverbs 2:6].

James 3:17 describes the wisdom that God imparts to us.

But the wisdom from above is first pure, then peaceable, gentle, reasonable, full of mercy and good fruits, unwavering, without hypocrisy.

12) GOD IS AWARE AND ATTENTIVE

We feel more confident and at peace after we have expressed our needs and concerns to God in prayer. God always graciously listens even though he is already fully aware of our situation and our concerns. Psalm 139:1−4 describes this so movingly.

> O Lord, You have searched me and known me.
> You know when I sit down and when I rise up;
> You understand my thought from afar.
> You scrutinize my path and my lying down,
> And are intimately acquainted with all my ways.
> Even before there is a word on my tongue,
> Behold, O Lord, You know it all.

Jesus said that God cares about even the smallest details of our lives. Knowing that helps us realize that he is even more attentive to our most important concerns.

> Are not two sparrows sold for a cent? And yet not one of them will fall to the ground apart from your Father. But the very hairs of your head are all numbered [Matthew 10:29−30].

God continually watches over us. He is our ever-present helper and protector.

2-14

PATIENT, JUST, AND MERCIFUL

13) GOD IS PATIENT

First Corinthians 13:4a says that love is patient. God's patience with us is one of the traits of the love that he has for us. Romans 2:4 links God's patience for us to his kindness toward us.

Or do you think lightly of the riches of His kindness and tolerance and patience, not knowing that the kindness of God leads you to repentance?

Patience is characterized by a willingness to wait. God is never hasty to punish sins, even though some people believe he is. Instead, God is patient as he encourages us to repent, turn to him, accept his free gifts of salvation and forgiveness, and enjoy the wonderful benefits of living in his kingdom.

The Lord is not slow about His promise, as some count slowness, but is patient toward you, not wishing for any to perish but for all to come to repentance [2 Peter 3:9].

And regard the patience of our Lord as salvation; just as also our beloved brother Paul, according to the wisdom given him, wrote to you [2 Peter 3:15].

The Bible says that God is slow to anger, which is another way of saying that he is patient. The restraint he shows when someone tries to provoke him is an aspect of his patience.

The Lord is slow to anger and great in power [Nahum 1:3a].

14) GOD IS JUST

God is just, fair, and honorable in all of his dealings with us. God's justice is closely associated with his righteousness and his lovingkindness.

He loves righteousness and justice;
The earth is full of the lovingkindness of the Lord [Psalm 33:5].

"But let him who boasts boast of this, that he understands and knows Me, that I am the Lord who exercises lovingkindness, justice and righteousness on earth; for I delight in these things," declares the Lord [Jeremiah 9:24].

God's justice, lovingkindness, righteousness, and truth are foundational to his kingship.

Righteousness and justice are the foundation of Your throne;
Lovingkindness and truth go before You [Psalm 89:14].

When God executes justice, he does it with graciousness and compassion. He is not like that reluctantly. He delights in being that way.

> Therefore the Lord longs to be gracious to you, and therefore He waits
> on high to have compassion on you. For the Lord is a God of justice;
> how blessed are all those who long for Him [Isaiah 30:18].

There were a small number of occasions when God punished a group of people for their long-standing evil behavior. Those incidents included the flood in the time of Noah in Genesis 5, the destruction of the cities of Sodom and Gomorrah in Genesis 18–19, the Egyptian plagues in Exodus 7–14, the overthrow and exile of Israel in 2 Kings 17, and the overthrow and exile of Judah in 2 Kings 25. There were also rare occasions when God punished individuals for particularly significant and potentially far-reaching sins. Examples included Adam and Eve in Genesis 3, Korah and his associates in Numbers 16, and Ananias and Sapphira in Acts 5. Partly based on those few incidents, many people have the mistaken belief that God is a God of vengeance and wrath and that he is constantly on the lookout for opportunities to judge and punish people. The truth is very different. He is a God who is always ready to forgive.

> For You, Lord, are good, and ready to forgive,
> And abundant in lovingkindness to all who call upon You [Psalm 86:5].

15) GOD IS MERCIFUL

In Exodus 25:10–22 God gave Moses detailed instructions for building the Ark of the Covenant. It would house the Ten Commandments which God had written on stone tablets. Most of us have probably never learned much about the ark's lid, which God called "the mercy seat." The ark itself was made of wood overlaid with gold; however, the mercy seat was made of solid gold. It was also decorated with two solid gold cherubim. Whenever Moses entered the tabernacle and met with God, God spoke to him, not from within the ark, but from between those cherubim on the mercy seat (Numbers 7:89). On the Day of Atonement, the high priest entered the Holy of Holies and sprinkled the blood of the sacrifices, not on the tablets or on the ark itself, but on the mercy seat (Leviticus 16). In the same way that the mercy seat was the focus of the priestly duties, God's mercy overshadows his law. He is a God of mercy, not a God of judgment.

But You, O Lord, are a God merciful and gracious,
Slow to anger and abundant in lovingkindness and truth [Psalm 86:15].

One of the most important ways that God shows his mercy to us is by releasing us from the consequences of our sins.

For God did not send the Son into the world to judge the world, but that the world might be saved through Him [John 3:17].

But God, being rich in mercy, because of His great love with which He loved us, even when we were dead in our transgressions, made us alive together with Christ [by grace you have been saved], and raised us up with Him, and seated us with Him in the heavenly places in Christ Jesus, so that in the ages to come He might show the surpassing riches of His grace in kindness toward us in Christ Jesus [Ephesians 2:4–7].

He saved us, not on the basis of deeds which we have done in righteousness, but according to His mercy, by the washing of regeneration and renewing by the Holy Spirit, whom He poured out upon us richly through Jesus Christ our Savior, so that being justified by His grace we would be made heirs according to the hope of eternal life [Titus 3:5–7].

In the same way that God has been merciful to us, we should be merciful to others.

Be merciful, just as your Father is merciful [Luke 6:36].

2-15

ALMIGHTY, MAJESTIC, SUPREME, ETERNAL, AND PERFECT

16) GOD IS ALMIGHTY

Three closely related terms—strength, power, and might—identify another of God's qualities. *Strength* makes possible the exertion of force. *Power* is the ability to act or produce an effect. *Might* is the power of which one is capable. God has unlimited strength, power, and might. He is almighty. Early in Genesis he represented himself to Abraham as God Almighty:

> Now when Abram was ninety-nine years old, the Lord appeared to Abram and said to him, "I am God Almighty; walk before Me, and be blameless" [Genesis 17:1].

The Bible closes with the reminder that God is and will always be almighty.

> I saw no temple in it, for the Lord God the Almighty and the Lamb are its temple [Revelation 21:22].

One summer day when my wife was a small child, she and some of her friends decided to build a playhouse. They found boards, nails, and a hammer. However, the task was beyond their design and construction ability. After hours of struggling with no meaningful progress, Brenda looked up and saw her father coming home from work. She jumped up and shouted, "Here comes big Walter! He'll help us!" And he did.

It is both awe-inspiring and comforting to realize that God is like that, but even better. It is awe-inspiring that his power is far greater than anything we can imagine. It is comforting that he cares for us and protects us and is always available to help us.

Because God is almighty, he has the ability and the power to do anything he chooses. Notice his questions to Abraham, Moses, and Jeremiah:

> Is anything too difficult for the Lord? [Genesis 18:14a].

> The Lord said to Moses, "Is the Lord's power limited?" [Numbers 11:23a].

> Behold, I am the Lord, the God of all flesh; is anything too difficult for Me? [Jeremiah 32:27].

The answers to those rhetorical questions are, of course, that the Lord's power is unlimited and nothing is too difficult for him. When Mary asked the angel Gabriel how she could conceive a son as a virgin, Gabriel replied:

> For nothing will be impossible with God [Luke 1:37].

Responding to a question from his disciples, Jesus told them that God is all-powerful.

> Looking at them, Jesus said, "With people it is impossible, but not with God; for all things are possible with God" [Mark 10:27].

The Bible addresses the magnitude of God's power on three levels: the cosmic level, the national level, and the personal level. At the cosmic level, God demonstrated his power in creation.

> Ah Lord God! Behold, You have made the heavens and the earth by Your great power and by Your outstretched arm! Nothing is too difficult for You [Jeremiah 32:17].

God demonstrated his power at the national level when he freed Israel from Egypt by causing the ten plagues, parting the Red Sea, and destroying Pharaoh's army when they pursued Israel.

> Moses said to the people, "Remember this day in which you went out from Egypt, from the house of slavery; for by a powerful hand the Lord brought you out from this place" [Exodus 13:3a].

But what is perhaps most relevant to us is that God demonstrates his power at the personal level on our behalf. There are three well-known instances of that in Jesus' ministry. In the first, God's power was present to heal people. In the second and third, God's power flowed through Jesus to heal people.

> One day He was teaching; and there were some Pharisees and teachers of the law sitting there, who had come from every village of Galilee and Judea and from Jerusalem; and the power of the Lord was present for Him to perform healing [Luke 5:17].

> And all the people were trying to touch Him, for power was coming from Him and healing them all [Luke 6:19].

> But Jesus said, "Someone did touch Me, for I was aware that power had gone out of Me" [Luke 8:46].

Not only does God employ his power on our behalf; he also imparts strength to us when we need it.

God is our refuge and strength,
A very present help in trouble [Psalm 46:1].

My help comes from the Lord,
Who made heaven and earth [Psalm 121:2].

He gives strength to the weary,
And to him who lacks might He increases power [Isaiah 40:29].

17) GOD IS MAJESTIC

Two qualities that uniquely belong to God are his majesty and his glory. Both are closely connected with the grandeur, beauty, radiance, and splendor of his appearance. Many passages in the Bible refer to God's majesty and glory, but only a few describe his appearance. Two of the best were written by Ezekiel in response to two separate visions. What Ezekiel saw was so glorious that he had difficulty adequately describing it.

It came about in the sixth year, on the fifth day of the sixth month, as I was sitting in my house with the elders of Judah sitting before me, that the hand of the Lord God fell on me there. Then I looked, and behold, a likeness as the appearance of a man; from His loins and downward there was the appearance of fire, and from His loins and upward the appearance of brightness, like the appearance of glowing metal [Ezekiel 8:1–2].

Now it came about in the thirtieth year, on the fifth day of the fourth month, while I was by the river Chebar among the exiles, the heavens were opened and I saw visions of God...

Now above the expanse that was over their [the cherubim's] heads there was something resembling a throne, like lapis lazuli in appearance; and on that which resembled a throne, high up, was a figure with the appearance of a man. Then I noticed from the appearance of His loins and upward something like glowing metal that looked like fire all around within it, and from the appearance of His loins and downward I saw something like fire; and there was a radiance around Him. As the appearance of the rainbow in the clouds on a rainy day, so was the appearance of the surrounding radiance. Such was the appearance of the likeness of the glory of the Lord. And when I saw it, I fell on my face and heard a voice speaking [Ezekiel 1:1, 26–28].

Daniel also saw a vision of God and had difficulty adequately describing it.

> I kept looking
> Until thrones were set up,
> And the Ancient of Days took His seat;
> His vesture was like white snow
> And the hair of His head like pure wool.
> His throne was ablaze with flames,
> Its wheels were a burning fire [Daniel 7:9].

Furthermore, John's description of his vision of the glorified Jesus is remarkably similar to what Ezekiel and Daniel saw in their visions.

> Then I turned to see the voice that was speaking with me. And having turned I saw seven golden lampstands; and in the middle of the lampstands I saw one like a son of man, clothed in a robe reaching to the feet, and girded across His chest with a golden sash. His head and His hair were white like white wool, like snow; and His eyes were like a flame of fire. His feet were like burnished bronze, when it has been made to glow in a furnace, and His voice was like the sound of many waters. In His right hand He held seven stars, and out of His mouth came a sharp two-edged sword; and His face was like the sun shining in its strength [Revelation 1:12–16].

If we saw a vision of God or of the glorified Jesus, we would be at a loss for adequate words to describe them, just as Ezekiel, Daniel, and John were.

In addition to times when God allowed his image to be seen, there were several occasions during which he revealed his glory to people.

> Then Moses went up to the mountain, and the cloud covered the mountain. The glory of the Lord rested on Mount Sinai, and the cloud covered it for six days; and on the seventh day He called to Moses from the midst of the cloud. And to the eyes of the sons of Israel the appearance of the glory of the Lord was like a consuming fire on the mountain top [Exodus 24:15–17].

> As I [Ezekiel] looked, behold, a storm wind was coming from the north, a great cloud with fire flashing forth continually and a bright light around it, and in its midst something like glowing metal in the midst of the fire [Ezekiel 1:4].

> But being full of the Holy Spirit, he [Stephen] gazed intently into heaven
> and saw the glory of God, and Jesus standing at the right hand of God
> [Acts 7:55].

God also reveals his glory to us through his creation. The Hubble telescope has recently provided us with stunning images of galaxies, stars, planets, and moons. As the psalmist wrote,

> The heavens are telling of the glory of God;
> And their expanse is declaring the work of His hands [Psalm 19:1].

Some people see God's glory most readily in biology: the amazing beauty, complexity, and diversity of plant, animal, bird, and marine life. Others see it most easily in music or literature or mathematics or in a newborn baby. Still others see it in personal relationships or in the transformed lives of people.

The seraphim near God's throne continually declare,

> Holy, Holy, Holy, is the Lord of hosts,
> The whole earth is full of His glory [Isaiah 6:3b].

God is glorious and majestic far beyond our comprehension. His magnificent appearance is a visible expression of his innate holiness and perfection. His mighty acts also reveal his majesty as well as his awesome power.

18) GOD IS SUPREME

He is God Most High, a title by which Scripture refers to him numerous times.

> I will cry to God Most High,
> To God who accomplishes all things for me [Psalm 57:2].

> That they may know that You alone, whose name is the Lord,
> Are the Most High over all the earth [Psalm 83:18].

As the Most High, he is the absolute Lord of all creation, to the exclusion of any other deity.

Know therefore today, and take it to your heart, that the Lord, He is God in heaven above and on the earth below; there is no other [Deuteronomy 4:39].

For You are the Lord Most High over all the earth;
You are exalted far above all gods [Psalm 97:9].

King Nebuchadnezzar, the most powerful ruler of his day, after God had dealt with him, declared:

But at the end of that period, I, Nebuchadnezzar, raised my eyes toward heaven and my reason returned to me, and I blessed the Most High and praised and honored Him who lives forever; for His dominion is an everlasting dominion, and His kingdom endures from generation to generation [Daniel 4:34].

God is supreme. He is unique and there is no other like him.

Who is like You among the gods, O Lord? Who is like You, majestic in holiness, awesome in praises, working wonders? [Exodus 15:11].

There are no other works like his.
There is no one like You among the gods, O Lord,
Nor are there any works like Yours [Psalm 86:8].

For Your righteousness, O God, reaches to the heavens,
You who have done great things;
O God, who is like You? [Psalm 71:19].

And he is the only savior.

I, even I, am the Lord, and there is no savior besides Me [Isaiah 43:11].

19) GOD IS ETERNAL

Unlike his creation, which will age and decay over time and then will one day be renewed, God is eternal. He exists outside of time. He does not change, and he is without beginning or end.

Your years are throughout all generations.

Of old You founded the earth,
And the heavens are the work of Your hands.
Even they will perish, but You endure;
And all of them will wear out like a garment;
Like clothing You will change them and they will be changed.
But You are the same,
And Your years will not come to an end [Psalm 102:24b–27].

He is the everlasting God who lives forever and ever.

Before the mountains were born
Or You gave birth to the earth and the world,
Even from everlasting to everlasting, You are God [Psalm 90:2].

But the Lord abides forever [Psalm 9:7a].

His kingdom and his kingship are eternal.

Your kingdom is an everlasting kingdom,
And Your dominion endures throughout all generations [Psalm
    145:13].

The Lord shall reign forever and ever [Exodus 15:18].

God desires to give us eternal life, as well. And he does so when we agree to his terms. He is able to do it because he is almighty and he himself is eternal.

For God so loved the world, that He gave His only begotten Son, that whoever believes in Him shall not perish, but have eternal life [John 3:16].

For this is the will of My Father, that everyone who beholds the Son and believes in Him will have eternal life, and I Myself will raise him up on the last day [John 6:40].

What will eternal life be like? We will experience unbelievable joy.

In Your presence is fullness of joy;
In Your right hand there are pleasures forever [Psalm 16:11b].

During eternal life, we will have uninterrupted access to and fellowship with God and Jesus.

> This is eternal life, that they may know You, the only true God, and Jesus Christ whom You have sent [John 17:3].

> Father, I desire that they also, whom You have given Me, be with Me where I am, so that they may see My glory which You have given Me, for You loved Me before the foundation of the world [John 17:24].

We will have eternal bodies that do not have the limitations of our present-day earthly bodies.

> For we know that if the earthly tent which is our house is torn down, we have a building from God, a house not made with hands, eternal in the heavens. For indeed in this house we groan, longing to be clothed with our dwelling from heaven, inasmuch as we, having put it on, will not be found naked. For indeed while we are in this tent, we groan, being burdened, because we do not want to be unclothed but to be clothed, so that what is mortal will be swallowed up by life [2 Corinthians 5:1–4].

We will have eternal homes that God has prepared for us to live in.

> In My Father's house are many dwelling places; if it were not so, I would have told you; for I go to prepare a place for you. If I go and prepare a place for you, I will come again and receive you to Myself, that where I am, there you may be also [John 14:2–3].

> Surely goodness and lovingkindness will follow me all the days of my life, And I will dwell in the house of the Lord forever [Psalm 23:6].

20) GOD IS PERFECT

God lacks nothing. He is flawless. Everything about him is of the utmost excellence. He is entirely perfect.

The Bible points out the perfection of some of the things he has done. Psalm 18:30 tells us his ways are blameless, perfect. Deuteronomy 32:4 says his work is perfect. Psalm 19:7 and James 1:25 refer to his law as perfect, a law of liberty. Romans 12:2 speaks of his perfect will. Isaiah 25:1 tells us that he worked wonders, which he planned long before, with perfect faithfulness. James 1:17 says his gifts are perfect. And Matthew 5:43–48 speaks of his perfect love. What a delight and a privilege to have a God who is perfect in every way!

2-16

SUMMARY

What is God like and how does he behave toward us? He is holy, righteous, just, truthful, trustworthy, and faithful. He is all-powerful, majestic, and superior to every other being yet is kind, wise, gracious, generous, and merciful. He loves us more than we can imagine, is fully aware of and attentive to everything that affects us, is approachable and available, and is minimally demanding. God is perfect, unchanging, and eternal. Let us join Paul in praising God for who he is.

> Now to the King eternal, immortal, invisible, the only God, be honor and glory forever and ever. Amen [1 Timothy 1:17].

Section 3

GOD DESIRES INTIMATE FELLOWSHIP WITH US

3-1

INTRODUCTION

Incredibly, our relationship with God is not based on his authority over us. It is based on his great love for us and his desire for intimate fellowship with us.

> We have come to know and have believed the love which God has for us. God is love, and the one who abides in love abides in God, and God abides in him [1 John 4:16].

He invites us into fellowship based upon mutual love: his love for us and our love for him.

> You shall love the Lord your God with all your heart, and with all your soul, and with all your mind [Matthew 22:37b].

> The grace of the Lord Jesus Christ, and the love of God, and the fellowship of the Holy Spirit, be with you all [2 Corinthians 13:14].

Many people limit God's invitation to close fellowship in two ways: 1) by having an inadequate understanding and appreciation of his desire for fellowship with us and 2) by placing too low of a priority on having fellowship with him. God never forces a relationship upon us. He allows us to decide how distant or intimate our relationship with him will be. But the closer we draw to him, the more fully we can enter into the many benefits and privileges he has in store for us.

3-2

TO WHAT DEGREE IS GOD INVOLVED?

Except for assuring us that God is the all-powerful creator of everything that is, the Bible reveals little about his involvement in overseeing the universe. Stepping down to the national level, there are numerous accounts of his involvement in the affairs of Israel and Judah. For instance, in Joshua 6 he caused the walls of Jericho to collapse, enabling Israel to capture that seemingly impregnable city. In Joshua 7 he allowed Israel's army to be defeated because people in Israel had disobeyed him regarding the spoils taken from Jericho. In Daniel 7 and 8 he revealed information about major world empires that would arise. Although there are numerous other examples in the Bible of God intervening in the affairs of Israel and Judah, there are relatively few accounts of his intervening in the affairs of other nations.

What about God's involvement in natural disasters? It is true that God caused Noah's flood, the ten plagues in Egypt, and a drought that lasted for three and a half years during the time of Elijah. Excluding those, the Bible does not record him causing any natural disasters. People are wrong to blame him for earthquakes, hurricanes, tornadoes, and so on. These natural events happen because the earth is geologically active. But here's an interesting question to ponder: How many times has God intervened to prevent or mitigate natural disasters?

Let's focus next on God's involvement with the citizens of his kingdom at the personal level—our level. According to *America's Four Gods*, half of all Americans believe God is not involved in their lives. The other half believes he is highly involved. Perhaps both are right, and his degree of involvement with us depends on how much we want him to be involved. Rather than taking an "it seems to me" approach to this topic, let's see what the Bible says about the degree to which God cares about our physical, emotional, spiritual, and relationship needs. For many of us, these needs are organized in the following order of priority:

1. Our happiness
2. Our health
3. Our finances
4. Our immediate needs
5. Our relationships with others
6. Our spiritual growth
7. Our relationship with God

Most people's top priorities are their happiness, health, finances, and immediate needs. Their relationships with others, their spiritual growth, and their relationship with God are often of lesser concern.

What priority order do you suppose God has for us in these areas? Would you agree that his priorities are probably the opposite of ours? Our relationship with him and our spiritual growth are of great importance to him.

Our health, wealth, and happiness are of lesser importance. Unfortunately, many of us interpret God's concern for us in terms of the health, wealth, and happiness that we—and the people who are closest to us—are experiencing.

Failing to understand God's priorities can cause us to question his innate goodness and his loving concern for us and for others. Let's take a look at those seven areas from God's perspective, addressing them in what is likely his order of importance.

3-3

OUR RELATIONSHIP WITH GOD

Most of us interact with God on the basis of our opinion of him and the need we feel for him. The way we relate to him is mostly based on how we interpret his two primary roles. The first role is as our sovereign with us as his subjects. With few exceptions, his principal relationship with people in Old Testament times was as their sovereign. However, if we view him as similar to earthly rulers, we tend to understand him either as a distant God who is uninvolved with us, or as an authoritative God who is very much involved but in a negative way. Either of those views can cause us to have negative feelings about him.

God's second role is as our loving heavenly Father, the way he is portrayed in the New Testament. One of the most enlightening events in history occurred when Jesus came to earth and revealed that we can have a relationship with God as his greatly loved children. We are not merely subjects in his kingdom; we are sons and daughters of the King! Jesus added a completely new dimension to our relationship with God. People do not usually say that they love their king, although most people honor and respect him. But everyone loves, honors, and respects a father who truly loves them. While most people feel in awe of their king, almost no one expects to be friends with him. But we can enjoy friendship and fellowship with a loving father. People tend to limit conversations with their king to matters of great urgency or critical importance. But we can talk with a loving father about anything, no matter how seemingly insignificant. God is indeed our king, but he is also our Father. This means that he can provide not only the strength, authority, and power of a king but also the intimate fellowship of a loving and caring father.

Many of us are parents, and we have nurtured our relationship with our children. Those of us with more than one child have discovered that each child has a unique personality as well as his or her own distinctive needs. In fulfilling our responsibilities to love and protect our children and to help them develop their full potential, we may struggle to be fair. Being fair does not necessitate treating each child identically. Rather, we try to be what each child needs us to be in ways that the child can understand and accept. And, as each child matures, we find ourselves modifying and adjusting how we accomplish that.

God does the same with us. He continually nurtures his relationship with us. He treats us as unique, with our own distinctive emotional and developmental needs. Some of us may need to become more independent while others of us may need to learn greater dependence upon him. Some of us may need greater confidence and self-esteem while others of us may need more humility. We can trust that God is always doing what is best for us, as Jesus taught in the Sermon on the Mount.

> Or what man is there among you who, when his son asks for a loaf, will give him a stone? Or if he asks for a fish, he will not give him a snake, will he? If you then, being evil, know how to give good gifts to your children, how much more will your Father who is in heaven give what is good to those who ask Him! [Matthew 7:9–11].

There will, of necessity, be give and take in our relationship with God. He is who he is, and he will not violate his nature or his principles. However, he can and will adapt his approach toward us. Likewise, we are who we are, but we can learn to transform our thoughts, attitudes, and actions to enhance our relationship with him.

3-4

OUR SPIRITUAL GROWTH

Our relationship with God evolves as we grow spiritually. To illustrate, let's suppose we have talent for a team sport such as football or baseball. There are many things we will need if we are to excel at our chosen sport. We need training that will help us improve our strength, balance, muscle control, and endurance. We need good coaches who can teach us playing skills. We need to learn the rules, techniques, and strategies of the game. We need to join a team and learn to work skillfully and reliably with our teammates.

There are parallels between the way people develop athletically and the way they develop spiritually. Both require commitment and effort. It will help our spiritual growth greatly to have a pastor, church leader, or mature person who will guide, teach, and encourage us. We need to study the Bible and other inspirational materials and put into practice what we learn there. We need to learn to recognize and listen to God's voice, follow his leading, and spend time getting to know him better. We need to learn to work with others and help one another grow spiritually.

3-5

OUR RELATIONSHIP WITH OTHERS

Our relationship with others is a vital topic that we will address in more detail in the next two sections of this book: "How Should We Treat Fellow Citizens of God's Kingdom?" (section 4) and "How Should We Treat People Who Are Not Yet Citizens of God's Kingdom?" (section 5). Our overall objectives are quite simple to summarize. We are to love and fellowship with the other citizens of God's kingdom, love and fellowship with our neighbors, lead exemplary lives, and encourage and build one another up. We should aspire to demonstrate God's love for all people through our attitudes toward them and through deliberate acts of kindness, grace, and mercy toward them.

3-6

OUR IMMEDIATE NEEDS

Jesus directly addressed our immediate needs twice during his Sermon on the Mount. In Matthew 6:11, he told us when we pray to ask God to "give us this day our daily bread." When we make this request, we are focusing on God to supply us with the things we need. Jesus assured us that God knows our needs, and we can trust him to supply them.

For this reason I say to you, do not be worried about your life, as to what you will eat or what you will drink; nor for your body, as to what you will put on. Is not life more than food, and the body more than clothing? Look at the birds of the air, that they do not sow, nor reap nor gather into barns, and yet your heavenly Father feeds them. Are you not worth much more than they? And who of you by being worried can add a single hour to his life? And why are you worried about clothing? Observe how the lilies of the field grow; they do not toil nor do they spin, yet I say to you that not even Solomon in all his glory clothed himself like one of these. But if God so clothes the grass of the field, which is alive today and tomorrow is thrown into the furnace, will He not much more clothe you? You of little faith! Do not worry then, saying, "What will we eat?" or "What will we drink?" or "What will we wear for clothing?" For the Gentiles eagerly seek all these things; for your heavenly Father knows that you need all these things. But seek first His kingdom and His righteousness, and all these things will be added to you. So do not worry about tomorrow; for tomorrow will care for itself. Each day has enough trouble of its own [Matthew 6:25–34].

Jesus said that our first priority is to seek the kingdom of God. Then God's provisions will follow. His provisions constantly remind us of his kindness, generosity, grace, mercy, and loving concern for us.

3-7

OUR HEALTH

We seldom dwell on our health when we have it but desperately seek when it is lacking. The Apostle John greeted his friend Gaius by writing, "Beloved, I pray that in all respects you may prosper and be in good health, just as your soul prospers" (3 John 2). Many people have interpreted that verse to mean that God wants not only Gaius, but also us, to be healthy. Is that a valid supposition? We certainly hope so. But if it is, why are there times when we are not healthy? For some people, those times seem never-ending. As we grow older, we may reach a point beyond which we will never again be completely healthy. How do we reconcile that with what 3 John 2 says? To answer this question, we need to look at how physical health is referenced in Scripture as a whole.

During his earthly ministry Jesus often healed people. If healing people were not God's will, Jesus certainly would not have done it.

> Therefore Jesus answered and was saying to them, "Truly, truly, I say to you, the Son can do nothing of Himself, unless it is something He sees the Father doing; for whatever the Father does, these things the Son also does in like manner" [John 5:19].

Jesus said in John 14:10b that everything he spoke came from the Father. That included each time he said, "Be healed." Jesus demonstrated that God can and will intervene to help us to be healthy and not sick. Furthermore, Jesus never made anyone sick.

Let's examine two commonly raised questions about God's role in sickness. The first is: Does God make us sick or let us become sick to "teach us a lesson" when he is angry with us? I could find only part of one Bible verse which implied that he would. David wrote that he was sick because God was angry with him.

> There is no soundness in my flesh because of Your indignation [Psalm 38:3a].

Since that is the only such instance in the entire Bible, we can safely rule out the misperception that God causes us or allows us to become sick because he is angry with us.

The second question is: Does God allow us to become sick to punish us for sinning? The second half of that same verse implies that he did such a thing to David.

> There is no health in my bones because of my sin [Psalm 38:3b].

Proverbs 3:7-8 implies the same thing:

> Do not be wise in your own eyes; fear the Lord and turn away from evil.
> It will be healing to your body and refreshment to your bones.

There is also the case of the paralyzed man in Matthew 9:2–7. Jesus implied that his sins had contributed to his becoming sick. Jesus then forgave the man's sins and healed him. That story provides a pattern for what we can do if we believe God has allowed us to become sick because we have sinned. There are two steps for us to take. The first is to confess our sins to God and ask his forgiveness. First John 1:9 assures us that he will forgive us whenever we ask him. The second step is to pray, asking God to heal us. Alternatively as James 5:14–16 counsels, we can ask someone else to pray for us.

Although sin can be associated with sickness, Jesus also pointed out to his disciples that sin cannot always be blamed when someone is in poor health. Sometimes God may choose to use the sickness for a greater purpose.

> As He passed by, He saw a man blind from birth. And His disciples asked Him, "Rabbi, who sinned, this man or his parents, that he would be born blind?" Jesus answered, "It was neither that this man sinned, nor his parents; but it was so that the works of God might be displayed in him" [John 9:1–3].

In addition, we need to take into account that our actions or inaction can contribute to improving, preserving, or damaging our health. We may unfairly blame God for health problems that we have brought upon ourselves. For instance, we are encouraged from many quarters to exercise, not to smoke, to avoid recreational drugs and excessive alcohol consumption, to eat right and maintain our weight at a healthy level, to reduce the stress in our lives, and to get sufficient rest and sleep. Actions like those contribute toward our being healthier. And when we are healthy, we can more easily resist infections and diseases and recover from injuries.

Finally, we need to remember that our bodies operate under the laws of nature. Some of us have bodies that have been injured in accidents, infected by outside agents, or impacted by genetic conditions. Such things also affect our health.

In conclusion, God did not promise we would never become sick. But when we do, he has provided multiple means by which we can be healed and restored to health. Those include our body's own built-in healing capabilities, prayers by us or on our behalf, and the Holy Spirit's gifts of healing. They also include doctors, surgery, and medications. In spite of these provisions, there may still be times when we desire to be healed but are not.

3-8

OUR FINANCES

Near the top of our priority list, but much lower on God's, are our finances. Returning to 3 John 2 we read, "Beloved, I pray that in all respects you may prosper and be in good health, just as your soul prospers." What does it mean for us to prosper? The first definition that pops into most people's minds is to thrive financially. Is it acceptable to God for us to prosper financially? The answer is definitely yes, but it is not an unconditional yes.

The theme verse of my book *Heaven's Success Secrets* is Jeremiah 29:11, which says,

> "For I know the plans that I have for you," declares the Lord, "plans for welfare and not for calamity to give you a future and a hope."

In that context, "welfare" includes health, happiness, prosperity, and well-being. Earlier in that same passage, Jeremiah wrote,

> Thus says the Lord of hosts, the God of Israel, to all the exiles whom I have sent into exile from Jerusalem to Babylon, "Build houses and live in them; and plant gardens and eat their produce. Take wives and become the fathers of sons and daughters, and take wives for your sons and give your daughters to husbands, that they may bear sons and daughters; and multiply there and do not decrease. Seek the welfare of the city where I have sent you into exile, and pray to the Lord on its behalf; for in its welfare you will have welfare" [Jeremiah 29:4–7].

Even though they were captives in a distant country and their situation was difficult, God instructed them to live active, productive lives. He ordered them to work, build houses, raise families, and start businesses. He told them to pray for the interests of their city as an avenue for improving their own situation. He encouraged them to prosper in their personal, family, and work lives, which is much more comprehensive than simply prospering financially. The Bible is timeless: That same message applies to us today.

God told Aaron to pronounce this blessing over people:

> The Lord bless you, and keep you;
> The Lord make His face shine on you, and be gracious to you;

The Lord lift up His countenance on you, and give you peace [Numbers 6:24–26].

God wants to be a continual source of blessing to us, just as he wanted to bless those Israelites long ago. Nevertheless, he does not promise to bless us apart from our relationship with him.

I love those who love me; and those who diligently seek me will find me. Riches and honor are with me, enduring wealth and righteousness. My fruit is better than gold, even pure gold, and my yield better than choicest silver. I walk in the way of righteousness, in the midst of the paths of justice, to endow those who love me with wealth, that I may fill their treasuries [Proverbs 8:17–21].

3-9

OUR HAPPINESS

If a genie suddenly appeared and offered to grant me a single wish, I would likely wish for perpetual happiness. Because of my personality type and temperament, that would be a highly optimistic request. And if it were granted me, there is always the danger there would be unintended negative consequences. Many of us remember how it turned out for the mythical King Midas, who was granted his wish that everything he touched would turn into gold.

Does God want us to be happy? Alternatively, does he want us to be unhappy? Or does he even care one way or the other? Those questions get to the heart of what many of us would like to gain from a relationship with God. The answers to these questions also affect the way we view our circumstances and our relationships with other people.

The word *unhappy* never appears in the Bible, so we can safely conclude that the answer to the question, "Does God want us to be unhappy?" is no. On the other hand, the Bible uses the word *happy* in the context of our questions in only a few verses in Psalms, Proverbs, and Ecclesiastes. For example,

How blessed is everyone who fears the Lord,
Who walks in His ways.
When you shall eat of the fruit of your hands,
You will be happy and it will be well with you [Psalm 128:1–2].

How blessed is the man who finds wisdom
And the man who gains understanding.
She is a tree of life to those who take hold of her,
And happy are all who hold her fast [Proverbs 3:13, 18].

He who despises his neighbor sins,
But happy is he who is gracious to the poor [Proverbs 14:21].

I have seen that nothing is better than that man should be happy in his
activities, for that is his lot [Ecclesiastes 3:22a].

Based on these verses, the answer to our first question, "Does God want
us to be happy?" is yes. Similarly, the answer to our third question, "Does
he care?" is also yes. Even so, our personal happiness is not one of the great
themes of the Bible. Don't be discouraged, though. We were not asking the
right questions. Let's look instead at three closely related concepts: joy,
enjoyment, and contentment.

Joy

In Scripture there are two types of joy. The first is *abiding joy*: a deep
imperturbable gladness. Abiding joy is internal and is independent of our
circumstances. That kind of joy is one of the benefits of our relationship
with God.

But the fruit of the Spirit is love, joy, peace, patience, kindness, goodness,
faithfulness, gentleness, self-control; against such things there is no law
[Galatians 5:22–23].

For the kingdom of God is not eating and drinking, but righteousness
and peace and joy in the Holy Spirit [Romans 14:17].

The second type of joy is *rejoicing*. Such joy can be our immediate
response to something that happens. At other times it may be when we
recognize that God has done something for us, perhaps answering one of
our prayers.

Until now you have asked for nothing in My name; ask and you will
receive, so that your joy may be made full [John 16:24].

Paul pronounced a blessing of joy upon us.

Now may the God of hope fill you with all joy and peace in believing, so that you will abound in hope by the power of the Holy Spirit [Romans 15:13].

Jude did as well.

Now to Him who is able to keep you from stumbling, and to make you stand in the presence of His glory blameless with great joy... [Jude 24].

There is much more joy to experience beyond this present life. We can look forward to a joyful future with the Lord.

And the ransomed of the Lord will return and come with joyful shouting to Zion, with everlasting joy upon their heads. They will find gladness and joy, and sorrow and sighing will flee away [Isaiah 35:10].

Enjoyment

Another concept that is closely related to happiness is enjoyment: pleasure, delight, exhilaration. The book of Ecclesiastes encourages us to enjoy life.

There is nothing better for a man than to eat and drink and tell himself that his labor is good. This also I have seen that it is from the hand of God. For who can eat and who can have enjoyment without Him? [Ecclesiastes 2:24–25].

Go then, eat your bread in happiness and drink your wine with a cheerful heart; for God has already approved your works. Let your clothes be white all the time, and let not oil be lacking on your head. Enjoy life with the woman whom you love all the days of your fleeting life which He has given to you under the sun; for this is your reward in life and in your toil in which you have labored under the sun [Ecclesiastes 9:7–9].

Contentment

Contentment is another closely related concept. Contentment can mean satisfaction, gratification, or serenity. All three are wonderful. Here are some encouraging verses about contentment:

Not that I speak from want, for I have learned to be content in whatever circumstances I am [Philippians 4:11].

But godliness actually is a means of great gain when accompanied by contentment. For we have brought nothing into the world, so we cannot take anything out of it either. If we have food and covering, with these we shall be content [1 Timothy 6:6–8].

Make sure that your character is free from the love of money, being content with what you have; for He Himself has said, "I will never desert you, nor will I ever forsake you" [Hebrews 13:5].

Although the Bible rarely speaks of our happiness, it speaks often about our joy, enjoyment, and contentment. That is indeed encouraging.

3-10

SUMMARY

What kind of relationship do we want with God? He is our King, but he is also our Father. We can have a close, personal relationship with him as our loving heavenly Father if we so desire. Two-way communication with him is foundational to such a relationship. It enables us to spend time getting to know one another better and discussing thoughts, ideas, plans, and issues. Another important aspect of fellowship with the Father is participating together in joint activities. Such a relationship has many advantages, including that he will be involved and can help us in all of our personal priorities:

1. Our relationship with him
2. Our spiritual growth and development
3. Our relationships with others
4. Our immediate needs
5. Our finances
6. Our health
7. Our happiness

As Jesus counseled us in Matthew 6:33,

But seek first His kingdom and His righteousness, and all these things will be added to you.

Section 4

HOW SHOULD WE TREAT FELLOW CITIZENS OF GOD'S KINGDOM?

4-1

INTRODUCTION

In Ephesians 3:14–19, Paul prayed that we might comprehend the extraordinary love that God has for us. He loves us so much that our minds can hardly grasp it. He also loves each of his other children that much. As God's children, we share the same heavenly Father and we live together in God's kingdom. We have a special relationship with one another: we are brothers and sisters in Christ, not only now but forever. In the light of our shared relationship, how should we treat one another? That is the topic of this section. To briefly summarize, we are to:

- Love one another.
- Pray for one another.
- Maintain unity.
- Encourage one another.
- Help one another.
- Accept one another.
- Forgive one another.

4-2

LOVE ONE ANOTHER

We need people in our lives to love. We also need people in our lives who love us—people who care about us, accept us, appreciate us, and consider us worthy of their love. God built those needs into us. Jesus provided straight-forward guidance about loving fellow citizens of the kingdom of God.

A new commandment I give to you, that you love one another, even as I have loved you, that you also love one another [John 13:34].

He repeated those instructions in John 15:12.

This is My commandment, that you love one another, just as I have loved you.

God loves us, but we normally find it hard to love God until we get to know him. Likewise, it is normally hard to love other people until we get to know them. In the verses we just read, Jesus was talking to his closest disciples during the Last Supper, right before his arrest, trial, and crucifixion. Those men were not mere acquaintances. They had spent three years traveling together and being mentored by Jesus. They had ministered together and knew each other well. Now that they knew each other, Jesus told them to love one another.

The word that Jesus used for *love* is the Greek word *agape*. *Agape* is the kind of unselfish, giving love that God has for us. It is the kind of love that we should seek to have for one another. Love like that does not arise effortlessly. It grows as we share interests and experiences, get to know one another, and develop mutual concern and respect for each other. That seems like a noble aim, but how do we go about achieving it?

As we increase in faith, we become people who can give and receive unselfish, sacrificial love. Even so, we cannot develop mutual agape relationships by ourselves. Those kinds of relationships require a combined effort by everyone involved. Our progress toward achieving mutual agape love will be highly influenced by two factors: our commitment to one another and the amount of quality time we spend together.

There are three essential attributes that we must cultivate if we want to develop mutual agape relationships with people.

1) We must become open and honest with them about who we are and what we are really like.

2) We must become good listeners and exhibit a genuine desire to get to know them.

3) We must be safe for them to confide in. This includes being non-judgmental about their thoughts, ideas, plans, issues, and problems. They must be able to trust that we will hold whatever information they share with us in complete confidence.

Acts 20:35 quotes Jesus as having said that it is more blessed to give than to receive. Keeping that in mind, we should take the initiative when it comes to loving others. We should try to make it easy for them to accept and respond to our love. And we should graciously accept the love they offer us. Loving one another includes both giving and receiving love.

When we love someone, we naturally seek ways to express that love to them. There are numerous ways to do that. The Golden Rule says to do for others the things we want them to do for us. Believing that, we normally express our love for someone in ways that are comfortable to us, ways that would feel like love to us. And we tend to interpret someone else's expressions of love for us in the light of our own love needs. But each person has unique love needs that have been shaped by a unique personality and life history. The result can be that one person's expressions of love may not seem like love at all to the other person. The other person might fail to even notice. Or they might interpret those efforts simply as courteous— or even thoughtless—gestures. When that happens, it can even create misunderstandings.

As an example, one day when I wasn't at home, my wife cleaned the garage and "organized my tools for me." I first noticed it when I was in the middle of a project and couldn't find some of the tools I needed. She had moved them to a different place in the garage and had put them inside a covered box. It even took her a while to find them. What she had intended as an act of love, I initially interpreted as somewhere between thoughtlessness and malice. So I offered to organize her kitchen for her sometime when she wasn't at home (for which I later apologized).

Gary Chapman's book, *The Five Love Languages,* explains why such miscommunications and misunderstandings can easily happen. He presented his insights in the context of marriage, but they are valid for other relationships as well. His key revelation was that each of us has our own individual love needs. We interpret other people's expressions of love for us on that basis. He identified five categories that encompass most of the ways people express love. Those same categories include most people's love needs.

1) Words of affirmation—saying things that build people up, such as compliments, praise, words of appreciation, words of encouragement, and words that express our belief in them and that we care for them

2) Quality time—spending uninterrupted time with one another; participating in joint activities; talking about meaningful experiences; discussing ideas, thoughts, feelings, plans, and hopes in an accepting atmosphere

3) Gifts—giving and receiving objects

4) Acts of service—being helpful, doing things for someone because you know they like them, doing things for someone that they cannot do for themselves

5) Physical touch—a warm handshake, an acknowledging pat on the back, an encouraging arm around the shoulder, a sincere hug, a kiss on the cheek for a friend, physical intimacy with a spouse

If we want friendship to progress into a mutual agape relationship, we must learn to express our love for someone in ways that feel like love to them. One way to begin is to talk about the five love languages and ask how meaningful each one is to them. Another way is to express love in a variety of ways and see which ones they most respond to. Our goal is to learn how to more genuinely and effectively express and receive love. Let us love one another.

4-3

PRAY FOR ONE ANOTHER

One of the greatest privileges we have as citizens of God's kingdom is unlimited access to him in prayer. Prayer is intended to be two-way communication. We speak to God and he listens. Then we listen for his answers. Many people never do that second part. They may not even know it is possible. But when we reduce prayer to a monologue, we preclude ourselves from hearing God's answers to our prayers.

The Bible encourages us to pray continually, to pray about everything, and to pray with thanksgiving.

Pray without ceasing [1 Thessalonians 5:17].

Be anxious for nothing, but in everything by prayer and supplication with thanksgiving let your requests be made known to God [Philippians 4:6].

Devote yourselves to prayer, keeping alert in it with an attitude of thanksgiving [Colossians 4:2].

John instructed us to pray in alignment with God's will, assuring us that he hears us when we pray in that way.

> This is the confidence which we have before Him, that, if we ask anything according to His will, He hears us. And if we know that He hears us in whatever we ask, we know that we have the requests which we have asked from Him [1 John 5:14–15].

Paul wrote that when we pray, it should not be solely from our minds, but it should be with assistance from the Holy Spirit.

> In the same way the Spirit also helps our weakness; for we do not know how to pray as we should, but the Spirit Himself intercedes for us with groanings too deep for words; and He who searches the hearts knows what the mind of the Spirit is, because He intercedes for the saints according to the will of God [Romans 8:26–27].

As we pray "in the spirit," Paul also urges us to "petition for all the saints."

> With all prayer and petition pray at all times in the Spirit, and with this in view, be on the alert with all perseverance and petition for all the saints [Ephesians 6:18].

When we join with others to pray about specific issues or needs, Jesus told us to pray in unity and agreement.

> Again I say to you, that if two of you agree on earth about anything that they may ask, it shall be done for them by My Father who is in heaven. For where two or three have gathered together in My name, I am there in their midst [Matthew 18:19–20].

Many excellent books have been written over the years on the subject of prayer. Countless sermons have been preached about it. There are many facets to prayer and many types of prayers, but I will limit our focus to praying for one another. Paul often told people that he had been praying for them.

> We give thanks to God always for all of you, making mention of you in our prayers [1 Thessalonians 1:2].

I thank God, whom I serve with a clear conscience the way my forefathers did, as I constantly remember you in my prayers night and day [2 Timothy 1:3].

Besides praying for others during his private prayer time, Paul was alert for opportunities to pray with others.

Now there were at Antioch, in the church that was there, prophets and teachers: Barnabas, and Simeon who was called Niger, and Lucius of Cyrene, and Manaen who had been brought up with Herod the tetrarch, and Saul. While they were ministering to the Lord and fasting, the Holy Spirit said, "Set apart for Me Barnabas and Saul for the work to which I have called them." Then, when they had fasted and prayed and laid their hands on them, they sent them away [Acts 13:1–3].

When he had said these things, he [Paul] knelt down and prayed with them all. And they began to weep aloud and embraced Paul, and repeatedly kissed him, grieving especially over the word which he had spoken, that they would not see his face again. And they were accompanying him to the ship [Acts 20:36–38].

In his epistles, Paul often asked others to pray for him.

Praying at the same time for us as well, that God will open up to us a door for the word, so that we may speak forth the mystery of Christ, for which I have also been imprisoned [Colossians 4:3].

And pray on my behalf, that utterance may be given to me in the opening of my mouth, to make known with boldness the mystery of the gospel [Ephesians 6:19].

We should pray for others. And we should solicit their prayers, especially when we are facing a specific decision or need. When we are with others, there will often be opportunities to pray together, both for their needs and concerns and for ours. For example, the persecuted Christians prayed for strength in Acts 4:29–32a.

"And now, Lord, take note of their threats, and grant that Your bond-servants may speak Your word with all confidence, while You extend Your hand to heal, and signs and wonders take place through the name of Your holy servant Jesus." And when they had prayed, the place where they had gathered together was shaken, and they were all filled with the Holy Spirit and began to speak the word of God with boldness. And the congregation of those who believed were of one heart and soul.

The church also prayed for Peter when he was put in prison.

When he [Herod] saw that it pleased the Jews, he proceeded to arrest Peter also. Now it was during the days of Unleavened Bread. When he had seized him, he put him in prison, delivering him to four squads of soldiers to guard him, intending after the Passover to bring him out before the people. So Peter was kept in the prison, but prayer for him was being made fervently by the church to God [Acts 12:3–5].

James encouraged believers to gather together to pray for those who were sick.

Is anyone among you suffering? Then he must pray. Is anyone cheerful? He is to sing praises. Is anyone among you sick? Then he must call for the elders of the church and they are to pray over him, anointing him with oil in the name of the Lord; and the prayer offered in faith will restore the one who is sick, and the Lord will raise him up, and if he has committed sins, they will be forgiven him. Therefore, confess your sins to one another, and pray for one another so that you may be healed. The effective prayer of a righteous man can accomplish much [James 5:13–16].

Let us pray for one another.

4-4

MAINTAIN UNITY

Unity does not require that we all be or act the same. Neither does unity require that we agree on every point of doctrine. Unity is about working together in harmony and good will. It is about Christian friendship, in which we love one another, respect our differences, and cooperate in advancing God's kingdom.

Romans 12:18 tells us, "If possible, so far as it depends on you, be at peace with all men." Romans 14:19 says, "So then we pursue the things which make for peace and the building up of one another." The vital purpose for maintaining unity is so we may glorify God together.

> Now may the God who gives perseverance and encouragement grant you to be of the same mind with one another according to Christ Jesus, so that with one accord you may with one voice glorify the God and Father of our Lord Jesus Christ. Therefore, accept one another, just as Christ also accepted us to the glory of God [Romans 15:5–7].

Establishing and maintaining unity means, first of all, that we each move from a self-focused view to a kingdom-of-God view of the world:

> Do nothing from selfishness or empty conceit, but with humility of mind regard one another as more important than yourselves; do not merely look out for your own personal interests, but also for the interests of others [Philippians 2:3–4].

We are each greatly loved and highly valued by God. When we understand that, it becomes easier to refrain from seeking honor and recognition for ourselves. It becomes easier to value others more highly and to look out for their interests in our interactions with them.

> And coming to Him as to a living stone, rejected by men, but choice and precious in the sight of God, you also, as living stones, are being built up as a spiritual house for a holy priesthood, to offer up spiritual sacrifices acceptable to God through Jesus Christ [1 Peter 2:4–5].

In these verses, Peter referred to Jesus, and to us, as living stones that are used to build a spiritual house. This description is a very effective metaphor for how to cooperate and build unity. For example, imagine a castle in Europe that is made of natural stones that come in many different shapes and sizes. When building with natural stones, construction workers have to take into consideration each stone's size, shape, and color pattern. In contrast, in the United States we almost never construct buildings of stones. Instead, we commonly build with bricks or concrete blocks. They are much easier to work with than stones because they are the same size, shape, color, and strength. They are completely interchangeable.

God does not make people like bricks or concrete blocks—each one exactly the same, each one fully interchangeable. We are unique, having our own appearance, abilities, interests, strengths, and weaknesses. In the same way that no two stones are identical, no two people are identical.

To achieve and maintain unity, we must recognize and appreciate one another's talents, abilities, strengths, weaknesses, and God-intended roles. God created us to be parts of the body of Christ, joined together into something much greater than we can be separately.

Peter made an interesting point when he called us "living" stones. As "living" stones, we can adapt to and accommodate the other people to whom we are joined. Paul provided a very good overview about the role of some of the different "living stones" in God's kingdom. In particular, God assigns some people to help others grow spiritually and learn how to function in his kingdom.

> And He gave some as apostles, and some as prophets, and some as evangelists, and some as pastors and teachers, for the equipping of the saints for the work of service, to the building up of the body of Christ; until we all attain to the unity of the faith, and of the knowledge of the Son of God, to a mature man, to the measure of the stature which belongs to the fullness of Christ [Ephesians 4:11–13].

What magnificent objectives those verses give us: unity of the faith, an ever-deepening understanding of who Jesus is, and a lifetime of maturing into Jesus' likeness. As we each do our part, the body of Christ will be further built up, to the benefit of us all.

4-5

ENCOURAGE ONE ANOTHER

D o you ever need a word of encouragement? I often do. Do you appreciate it when someone offers you encouragement? I certainly do. When we encourage people, we inspire them with hope, courage, and confidence.

Jesus is an encourager. Jesus' words inspire our hope, courage, and confidence. At the Last Supper, he inspired hope in his disciples by encouraging them to look beyond the events of the next few days and take a kingdom-of-God perspective toward the future.

> "Do not let your heart be troubled; believe in God, believe also in Me.
> ...I go to prepare a place for you" [John 14:1–2].

He inspired their courage by promising that his peace would remain upon them.

> "Peace I leave with you; My peace I give to you; not as the world gives
> do I give to you. Do not let your heart be troubled, nor let it be fearful"
> [John 14:27].

He inspired their confidence by promising that he and the Father would jointly send the Holy Spirit to be both with them and in them.

> I will ask the Father, and He will give you another Helper, that He may
> be with you forever; that is the Spirit of truth, whom the world cannot
> receive, because it does not see Him or know Him, but you know Him
> because He abides with you and will be in you [John 14:16–17].

After Jesus ascended, the Holy Spirit became the disciples' ever-present helper, comforter, and encourager. The Holy Spirit taught them. The Holy Spirit helped them recall what Jesus had said during his earthly ministry (John 14:26). The Holy Spirit testified about Jesus, both to them and through them (John 15:26–27). Today God speaks to us, instructs us, and encourages us both through the Bible and through the Holy Spirit (John 16:13). What the Holy Spirit did for the first disciples, he does for us when we learn to hear him speak through Scripture and through his quiet voice within us.

In addition to Jesus' words and the Holy Spirit's encouragement, we also need people to encourage, exhort, and reassure us. These people may be our parents, our spouses, our pastors, Bible teachers, Sunday school teachers, or close friends. If we will make ourselves transparent to them, they will be better able to sense when we need their encouragement. We need to accept their words of encouragement, knowing that they offer them because of their love for us.

One of the ways we can convey our love to someone is through affirming them with words of acceptance, encouragement, support, and comfort. First Thessalonians 5:11 urges us to encourage one another and build one another up. Scripture means this to be a reciprocal act, for we need both to offer and to accept encouragement. Hebrews 10:24 tells us to think of ways to stimulate one another to love and good deeds. One way to do that is by voicing our appreciation for their talents, abilities, gifts, good attitudes, strengths, and good deeds. Another is to encourage them to use their God-given talents, abilities, and gifts to help others.

To become effective encouragers, it is important that we learn to listen to the quiet inner voice of the Holy Spirit whenever he speaks to us. He knows when someone needs encouraging, and he knows what sort of encouragement they need. It might be that the best way to encourage them is to express our love and appreciation. It might be to share some specific Bible verses that provide the insight they need, or to challenge them to trust God in practical ways. We must become willing to "take a risk" and respect our inner urgings to encourage someone. It could be exactly what they need at the moment.

4-6

HELP ONE ANOTHER

B ecause God is available to help us, Jesus is available to help us, and the Holy Spirit is available to help us, we are liberated to help others with their needs.

When we help someone, we are investing our time and effort in doing things for them that they either do not know how to do or are unable to do. James encouraged us to help people in practical ways, especially if they are fellow citizens of the kingdom of God.

> If a brother or sister is without clothing and in need of daily food, and one of you says to them, "Go in peace, be warmed and be filled," and yet you do not give them what is necessary for their body, what use is that? [James 2:15-16].

"Treat others the same way you want them to treat you" (Luke 6:31) is a fitting verse for our context. We want people to help us when we are in need, so we should be alert for opportunities help other people who are in need. In the same way, it is important that those being helped are respectful of the time, efforts, and resources of those helping them.

We each have strengths, skills, and areas of knowledge and proficiency. Paul encouraged us to use those abilities to help others.

So then, while we have opportunity, let us do good to all people, and especially to those who are of the household of the faith [Galatians 6:10].

Jesus taught that the true leaders are the ones who help and serve others:

Whoever wishes to become great among you shall be your servant, and whoever wishes to be first among you shall be your slave [Matthew 20:26–27].

Paul was an excellent example of that.

You yourselves know that these hands ministered to my own needs and to the men who were with me. In everything I showed you that by working hard in this manner you must help the weak and remember the words of the Lord Jesus, that He Himself said, "It is more blessed to give than to receive" [Acts 20:34–35].

Another way to help others is to cooperate with the Holy Spirit, allowing him to impart his gifts through you to help those who need a word or a touch from him. If you are one of those people, Peter wrote this to you:

As each one has received a special gift, employ it in serving one another as good stewards of the manifold grace of God. Whoever speaks, is to do so as one who is speaking the utterances of God; whoever serves is to do so as one who is serving by the strength which God supplies; so that in all things God may be glorified through Jesus Christ, to whom belongs the glory and dominion forever and ever. Amen [1 Peter 4:10–11].

It is essential to minister the Holy Spirit's gifts with an attitude of love.

For you were called to freedom, brethren; only do not turn your freedom into an opportunity for the flesh, but through love serve one another [Galatians 5:13]. [See also 1 Corinthians 13.]

We are able to help others because God is there to help us. If you ever feel as if there is no one to help you, you can be immediately encouraged by looking at the promises God has given in the Scripture.

For I am the Lord your God, who upholds your right hand, who says to you, "Do not fear, I will help you" [Isaiah 41:13].

God is our refuge and strength, a very present help in trouble [Psalm 46:1].

He is available with help for us whenever we ask him.

I will lift up my eyes to the mountains; from where shall my help come? My help comes from the Lord, who made heaven and earth [Psalm 121:1–2].

The Lord is near to all who call upon Him, to all who call upon Him in truth [Psalm 145:18].

During Jesus' earthly ministry, people who had no other hope turned to him for help.

And a leper came to Him and bowed down before Him, and said, "Lord, if You are willing, You can make me clean." Jesus stretched out His hand and touched him, saying, "I am willing; be cleansed." And immediately his leprosy was cleansed [Matthew 8:2–3].

And large crowds came to Him, bringing with them those who were lame, crippled, blind, mute, and many others, and they laid them down at His feet; and He healed them [Matthew 15:30].

When Jesus returned to heaven, he did not leave us alone or helpless. As he had promised, God and he jointly sent the Holy Spirit to be our helper.

I will ask the Father, and He will give you another Helper, that He may be with you forever [John 14:16].

But the Helper, the Holy Spirit, whom the Father will send in My name, He will teach you all things, and bring to your remembrance all that I said to you [John 14:26].

4-7

ACCEPT ONE ANOTHER

Christ surely does not agree with all of my opinions, or with all of yours. I do not believe that he approves of every one of my actions, or of yours. But as the well-known invitation hymn says, we can come to God just as we are. God loves us and accepts us, in spite of our imperfections. Can we do the same for one another? Why should we allow anything to come between us?

Paul urged the Ephesians to show "tolerance for one another in love" (Ephesians 4:2). He also instructed the Colossians to "put on a heart of compassion, kindness, humility, gentleness, and patience, bearing with one another" (Colossians 3:12-13). That does not imply we have to agree with or approve of everything about one another. But it does mean that we should accept one another as brothers and sisters in Christ and as fellow citizens of the kingdom of God because we will spend eternity together with God.

> Therefore, accept one another, just as Christ also accepted us to the glory of God [Romans 15:7].

Whenever people gather together, there will be differences of opinion. In order to accept one another, we must tolerate our different opinions, our different priorities, and our different behaviors. For example, the church at Rome had two differences of opinion that were causing friction among God's people. (See Romans 14:1 through 15:7.) The issues were:
1) Which foods were acceptable to eat, and
2) How people should treat special days such as Sabbaths (Saturdays), Sundays, or other religious holidays.

Paul did not take sides on either of those issues. He gave each person the liberty to act according to their own conscience. He wrote that those on both sides of the issue should not judge those on the other side or hold them in contempt. Likewise, they shouldn't try to impose their own opinions and standards of behavior on others.

> The one who eats is not to regard with contempt the one who does not eat, and the one who does not eat is not to judge the one who eats, for God has accepted him [Romans 14:3].

We have to "cut one another some slack." We don't need to cast judgment on issues that don't have eternal significance. Let us accept one another.

4-8

FORGIVE ONE ANOTHER

We are not perfect people, and we do not live in a perfect world. Misunderstandings and misinterpretations occur. Slights and offenses happen, sometimes intentionally but more often unintentionally. What are we to do when misunderstandings, slights, or offenses affect our attitudes toward one another or impair our relationships with one another?

The answers are quite simple, but they may not be easy for us to do. When we are the offending party, it is our responsibility to go to those whom we have offended and confess, repent, and ask for their forgiveness. That is exactly the same thing that we are to do when we sin against God. "If we confess our sins, He is faithful and righteous to forgive us our sins and to cleanse us from all unrighteousness" (1 John 1:9). God forgives us when we ask him because it is his nature. "For You, Lord, are good, and ready to forgive, and abundant in lovingkindness to all who call upon You" (Psalm 86:5). Aren't we thankful he is that kind of God? And we hope the person to whom we have apologized will likewise forgive us.

When we are the offended party and someone comes to us, confesses, repents, and asks for our forgiveness, we are to respond as God would. We are to forgive them. Paul said that believers should "[bear] with one another, and [forgive] each other, whoever has a complaint against anyone; just as the Lord forgave you, so also should you" (Colossians 3:13).

Jesus said, "Whenever you stand praying, forgive, if you have anything against anyone, so that your Father who is in heaven will also forgive you your transgressions" (Mark 11:25). Thus Jesus said that God will forgive our transgressions against him to the same extent that we forgive other people's transgressions against us. If God forgives us when we ask him, how can we not do the same for others when they ask us?

Forgiveness and reconciliation are essential to restoring broken relationships when there has been an offense, whether real or imagined, whether intentional or unintentional. Let's look at two cases. Case 1: we were offended at what someone did or said, but they did not or would not come to us, confess, repent, and ask for forgiveness. Case 2: someone misconstrued something we said or did, or neglected to say or do, and took offense at us. Either case can cause a breach in a relationship. What are we to do? Jesus provided the answers in the Sermon on the Mount. God places a very high priority on mending a strained relationship, and in both cases we have a responsibility to make every effort to restore the relationship.

> Therefore if you are presenting your offering at the altar, and there remember that your brother has something against you, leave your offering there before the altar and go; first be reconciled to your brother, and then come and present your offering [Matthew 5:23–24].

Is there someone who continually "rubs you the wrong way," so that each time he does it you struggle to forgive him? Let me recommend a better way to handle it. God not only forgave your past sins, he also forgave you for being a sinner. By doing that, he no longer has to deal with each instance of your sinning. Why not do the same and forgive that person for having those faults? If you will do that, you will no longer have to deal with your emotions every time that person exhibits one of those faults.

As citizens of God's kingdom, we are obligated to forgive one another's faults because God has forgiven ours. "Above all, keep fervent in your love for one another, because love covers a multitude of sins" (1 Peter 4:8). In a similar way, Proverbs 10:12 says that love covers all transgressions. While my love for you cannot cover your sins against someone else, it certainly ought to cover whatever sins you commit against me.

Let me make one more significant point. As part of our growth as citizens of God's kingdom, we should be endeavoring to become people who are not easily offended, who are not easily angered, and who readily forgive others. "Be kind to one another, tender-hearted, forgiving each other, just as God in Christ also has forgiven you" (Ephesians 4:32).

Jesus quoted from the Old Testament to describe what our attitude should be toward others: "You shall love your neighbor as yourself" (Matthew 22:39). Our mutual love for God and our mutual love for one another are what unite us as citizens of God's kingdom. Our love for one another is to be our guiding principle for how we treat others and for how they treat us.

4-9

SUMMARY

How should we treat fellow citizens of the kingdom of God? We are to

- Love one another.
- Pray for one another.
- Maintain unity.
- Encourage one another.
- Help one another.
- Accept one another.
- Forgive one another.

So then let us pursue the things which make for peace and the building up of one another [Romans 14:19].

To sum up, all of you be harmonious, sympathetic, brotherly, kindhearted, and humble in spirit; not returning evil for evil or insult for insult, but giving a blessing instead; for you were called for the very purpose that you might inherit a blessing [1 Peter 3:8–9].

Section 5

HOW SHOULD WE TREAT PEOPLE WHO ARE NOT YET CITIZENS OF GOD'S KINGDOM?

5-1

INTRODUCTION

G od's attitude toward people is what determines how he treats them. So, we need to ask, "What is his attitude toward people?" To put it simply, God loves them, regardless of whether or not they are yet citizens of his kingdom. To God, every person is someone who needs to be saved, is worth saving, and is someone whom he deeply desires to save. Aren't we grateful that he felt that way about us when we were not yet citizens of his kingdom?

> For God so loved the world, that He gave His only begotten Son, that whoever believes in Him shall not perish, but have eternal life. For God did not send the Son into the world to judge the world, but that the world might be saved through Him [John 3:16–17].

God is continually reaching out to people with his love, mercy, and grace. Jesus illustrated that in the parable about the shepherd who sought a lost sheep (Luke 15:3–7) and the father who welcomed the prodigal son back home (Luke 15:11–24). The truth is that none of us can wander so far astray that we are beyond God's willingness to accept us when we repent and turn to him.

In the same way that God's attitude shapes the way he treats people, our attitude toward people shapes the way we treat them. Jesus taught that God calls believers to follow a higher standard of love than the world offers.

> "You have heard that it was said, 'You shall love your neighbor and hate your enemy.' But I say to you, love your enemies and pray for those who persecute you, so that you may be sons of your Father who is in heaven; for He causes His sun to rise on the evil and the good, and sends rain on the righteous and the unrighteous. For if you love those who love you, what reward do you have? Do not even the tax collectors do the same? If you greet only your brothers, what more are you doing than others? Do not even the Gentiles do the same? Therefore you are to be perfect, as your heavenly Father is perfect" [Matthew 5:43–48].

In what ways can we become perfect like our Father is? We can become perfect in our attitude toward people and in our love for people, whether or not they are yet citizens of God's kingdom.

Think about the time when you were not yet a citizen of God's kingdom. How were you treated by Christians—positively or negatively?

- Did someone take a personal interest in you because he or she was a citizen of God's kingdom?
- Or, did someone seem to dislike you or avoid you because you were not a citizen of God's kingdom?
- Did someone tell you about God and his kingdom in a convincingly positive way?
- Or, did someone try to frighten you about the possibility of your going to hell?
- Did someone model living in God's kingdom in a way that was attractive and appealing to you?

Before I was a believer, there were Sunday school teachers who took a personal interest in me and taught me about God in positive ways. I remember people who lived upright and moral lives. On the other hand, I also remember sermons that were aimed at frightening people about the reality of hell and the possibility of going there. I remember people who were like the Pharisees of Jesus' day, living in rigid conformity to a set of man-made rules against going to movies, playing cards, or dancing—activities that I regularly enjoyed and viewed as innocent fun. People like them tended to avoid anyone who did not view the world exactly as they did.

None of the influences to which I was exposed were sufficient to convince me to establish my own relationship with God. What I needed was to get to know someone who was living *inside* God's kingdom in a way that was more appealing than the way I was living *outside* of it. God graciously arranged for me to do that. I got to know a Methodist pastor who truly loved God and who exuded God's love for people—all people. Getting to know him melted my resistance and prepared me to commit and entrust my life to God. How did God bring you into his kingdom?

Let me ask some pointed questions about the message that we are sending to those who are not yet in God's kingdom:

- What is there in your and my attitude toward people that would attract someone to life in God's kingdom?
- What is there in your and my attitude that might repel people from God?

- Who might be watching you and me in order to make a decision about whether to follow God?

Because of what God has so graciously done for us, we must let others know that he can do the same for them. Our attitudes and our actions toward unbelievers should be such that they feel God's love through us and are thereby drawn to him. We too were once separated from Christ, were without God, and had no hope of eternal life (Ephesians 2:12). But now we are no longer strangers or aliens but citizens of God's kingdom, members of his own household (Ephesians 2:19). We should always be alert for opportunities to invite people to become fellow citizens with us of God's kingdom. Throughout the remainder of this section, we will consider specific actions we can take toward accomplishing those objectives.

5-2

LOVE YOUR NEIGHBOR

When my father died, I remember something that someone said at the funeral home during family visitation. A woman whose property adjoined my parents' property was there and offered her condolences. My mother introduced her to a family friend, saying "This is Sarah, my neighbor." Sarah replied, "No, we are not neighbors. We just live near one another." She was right. Neither Sarah nor my mother had been a neighbor to the other. They didn't "visit across the fence." They didn't go places together. Neither had visited in the other's home. And neither did anything to help the other when their husbands were terminally ill. They lived near each other, but they were not neighbors.

Jesus had a very interesting conversation about the definition of neighbor with one of the lawyers of his day.

> And a lawyer stood up and put Him [Jesus] to the test, saying, "Teacher, what shall I do to inherit eternal life?" And He said to him, "What is written in the Law? How does it read to you?" And he answered, "You shall love the Lord your God with all your heart, and with all your soul, and with all your strength, and with all your mind; and your neighbor as yourself." And He said to him, "You have answered correctly; do this

and you will live." But wishing to justify himself, he said to Jesus, "And who is my neighbor?" [Luke 10:25–29].

The lawyer must have thought he was very clever when he asked Jesus, "Who is my neighbor?" (Luke 10:29). I suspect that he wanted to define his neighbor very narrowly, as many of us may do. Probably everyone whom he counted as his neighbor was Jewish, of a similar age and social status, had similar values, observed religion with a similar degree of commitment, and held similar political views. In short, anyone he classified as a neighbor was someone just like him. Don't we often act the same way?

Jesus answered the lawyer's question by telling a parable that showed God's commandment to "love your neighbor as yourself" was much broader than the lawyer had hoped.

> Jesus replied and said, "A man was going down from Jerusalem to Jericho, and fell among robbers, and they stripped him and beat him, and went away leaving him half dead. And by chance a priest was going down on that road, and when he saw him, he passed by on the other side. Likewise a Levite also, when he came to the place and saw him, passed by on the other side. But a Samaritan, who was on a journey, came upon him; and when he saw him, he felt compassion, and came to him and bandaged up his wounds, pouring oil and wine on them; and he put him on his own beast, and brought him to an inn and took care of him. On the next day he took out two denarii and gave them to the innkeeper and said, 'Take care of him; and whatever more you spend, when I return I will repay you.' Which of these three do you think proved to be a neighbor to the man who fell into the robbers' hands?" And he [the lawyer] said, "The one who showed mercy toward him." Then Jesus said to him, "Go and do the same" [Luke 10:30–37].

This parable is even more meaningful when you remember that Jews and Samaritans had a centuries-old hatred for one another. The Samaritan chose to help a Jew, who was a total stranger and a member of a different religious group. Translated into a modern setting from a Western point of view, this parable might be about a Christian lying on the side of the road who was ignored by a Roman Catholic priest and an evangelical pastor and then rescued by a Muslim.

Who is my neighbor? According to Jesus, it is whomever I come into contact with. Jesus showed that the commandment to be a neighbor transcends nationalities. It transcends religious affiliations and worship styles. And it transcends political affiliations and opinions.

Who proved to be a neighbor to the man who was in desperate need? The lawyer agreed that it was the one who showed him mercy. Jesus instructed the lawyer to go and do the same. That applies to us as well. Paul wrote,

> Owe nothing to anyone except to love one another; for he who loves his neighbor has fulfilled the law. For this, "You shall not commit adultery, you shall not murder, you shall not steal, you shall not covet," and if there is any other commandment, it is summed up in this saying, "You shall love your neighbor as yourself." Love does no wrong to a neighbor; therefore love is the fulfillment of the law [Romans 13:8–10].

5-3

WHAT ABOUT OUR ENEMIES?

We normally consider those individuals and groups who hate us to be our enemies. The Old Testament concept was that if they hate us, we will hate them. If they seek our destruction, we will seek theirs. If they offend or harm us, we will retaliate. Modern-day Israel still seems to have that philosophy.

But Jesus said we must love our enemies, even that we should pray for them. That is in total opposition to most people's natural tendencies.

> You have heard that it was said, "You shall love your neighbor and hate your enemy." But I say to you, love your enemies and pray for those who persecute you, so that you may be sons of your Father who is in heaven; for He causes His sun to rise on the evil and the good, and sends rain on the righteous and the unrighteous [Matthew 5:43–45].

Love our enemies? Impossible! So what if God does? So what if he chooses to be kind to people who are unrighteous, evil, or have declared themselves to be his enemy? Does that mean that we have to behave like God does and love our enemies? Yes it does, if we are truly dedicated to doing what Jesus says, if we in fact want to be the kind of people that Jesus wants us to be.

Jesus clearly described what our responses should be to enemies.

> But I say to you who hear, love your enemies, do good to those who
> hate you, bless those who curse you, pray for those who mistreat you
> [Luke 6:27–28].

Do good to people who hate us? Bless people who curse us? Pray for
people who mistreat us? Surely Jesus didn't really mean for us to do that! But
he did! And that's not all that he taught.

> Whoever hits you on the cheek, offer him the other also; and whoever
> takes away your coat, do not withhold your shirt from him either. Give
> to everyone who asks of you, and whoever takes away what is yours,
> do not demand it back. Treat others the same way you want them to
> treat you. If you love those who love you, what credit is that to you? For
> even sinners love those who love them. If you do good to those who do
> good to you, what credit is that to you? For even sinners do the same.
> If you lend to those from whom you expect to receive, what credit is
> that to you? Even sinners lend to sinners in order to receive back the
> same amount. But love your enemies, and do good, and lend, expecting
> nothing in return; and your reward will be great, and you will be sons
> of the Most High; for He Himself is kind to ungrateful and evil men. Be
> merciful, just as your Father is merciful [Luke 6:29–36].

What is going on here? That scripture passage goes completely against
our desire for retaliation and revenge when we believe we have been wronged
or offended or cheated or taken advantage of. When we are confronted by
someone who hates us, it is totally unnatural to behave the way Jesus just
described.

What is going on here is that Jesus wants us to behave, not as the world
does, but as God does. Jesus wants us to conform, not to the world's standards of behavior, but to God's standards of behavior. We are to let our love
for others overcome their hostility and hatred toward us.

When someone wrongs them, most people experience a strong desire
to take revenge, which often leads to an escalation of the conflict. God calls
for citizens of his kingdom to stop this cycle. Paul wrote:

> Never pay back evil for evil to anyone. Respect what is right in the
> sight of all men. If possible, so far as it depends on you, be at peace
> with all men. Never take your own revenge, beloved, but leave room
> for the wrath of God, for it is written, "Vengeance is Mine, I will
> repay," says the Lord. "But if your enemy is hungry, feed him, and if he
> is thirsty, give him a drink; for in so doing you will heap burning coals

on his head." Do not be overcome by evil, but overcome evil with good [Romans 12:17–21].

When an offence occurs, the typical cycle is retaliation and revenge followed by continued retaliation and revenge. Breaking this cycle begins with those of us in the kingdom of God choosing to ignore offenses against us. It continues with seeking reconciliation with the offender rather than seeking vengeance. And it concludes with treating the offenders with kindness and mercy.

> See that no one repays another with evil for evil, but always seek after that which is good for one another and for all people [1 Thessalonians 5:15].

5-4

BE AN EXAMPLE

If you wanted to see what living in God's kingdom was supposed to look like, what would you do? You would probably watch some of the citizens of the kingdom as they go about their ordinary daily activities. You would notice their attitudes, how they conducted their activities, and the ways they interacted with people. As citizens of God's kingdom, we must continually show forth the light of his kingdom and do good works of a type that will attract people to God. Jesus taught:

> You are the light of the world. A city set on a hill cannot be hidden; nor does anyone light a lamp and put it under a basket, but on the lampstand, and it gives light to all who are in the house. Let your light shine before men in such a way that they may see your good works, and glorify your Father who is in heaven [Matthew 5:14–16].

When people watch you and me, what do they see? Far too often there is a discrepancy between ideal kingdom living and the version that we practice. Gandhi admired Jesus and often quoted from the Sermon on the Mount. The Reverend E. Stanley Jones, well-known missionary to India, once asked Gandhi why he so adamantly rejected becoming a follower of Jesus. Gandhi replied, "O, I don't reject Christ. I love Christ. It's just that so many of you Christians are so unlike Christ." Then Gandhi added, "If

Christians would really live according to the teachings of Christ, as found in the Bible, all of India would be Christian today." What an indictment of the way our wrong attitudes and actions can repulse people and cast an unfavorable light on God's kingdom!

Jesus said, "In everything, therefore, treat people the same way you want them to treat you, for this is the Law and the Prophets" (Matthew 7:12). We have already discussed our obligation to show God's love to the people we come into contact with. And we have discussed what Jesus and Paul taught about the way to treat enemies. So what else should we do to become lights to the world? Perhaps the best and most concise list of dos and don'ts can be found in Galatians 5. The don'ts:

> Now the deeds of the flesh are evident, which are: immorality, impurity, sensuality, idolatry, sorcery, enmities, strife, jealousy, outbursts of anger, disputes, dissensions, factions, envying, drunkenness, carousing, and things like these, of which I forewarn you, just as I have forewarned you, that those who practice such things will not inherit the kingdom of God [Galatians 5:19–21].

Read carefully through that list again and decide which of those characteristics, when displayed by citizens of God's kingdom, would attract people to God. My answer would be "none of them." And which of those characteristics would cast God's kingdom in a bad light? My answer would be "all of them." As citizens of God's kingdom, we must cease from all such deeds of the flesh, if for no other reason than because of the disparagement they bring upon God and upon his followers.

Next let's consider the dos.

> But the fruit of the Spirit is love, joy, peace, patience, kindness, goodness, faithfulness, gentleness, self-control; against such things there is no law [Galatians 5:22–23].

Are those attractive qualities to observe in people? They certainly are! The fruit of the Spirit epitomize the characteristics of an ideal citizen of God's kingdom. Let us live in such a way that people will see in us what living in God's kingdom is supposed to look like.

5-5

SUMMARY

We must let love direct our attitudes and actions, especially toward people who are not yet citizens of God's kingdom.

Section 6

JESUS' KINGDOM CREDENTIALS

6-1

INTRODUCTION

Jesus spent much of his earthly ministry teaching about and demonstrating the good news about the kingdom of God. There has never been, nor will there ever be, anyone else who could speak as authoritatively about the kingdom of God. That is true for two very significant reasons. First, he was relating what he had seen and done while he dwelled in heaven before coming to earth. Second, he was revealing what he would do when he returned to his place in heaven, which would include reigning over the kingdom of God. In this section, we will explore why Jesus was uniquely qualified to speak authoritatively about the kingdom of God. In section 7, we will study what he disclosed about it.

6-2

JESUS' GOOD NEWS ABOUT THE KINGDOM OF GOD

The first message that John the Baptist preached was, "Repent, for the kingdom of heaven is at hand" (Matthew 3:2). Likewise, the first message that Jesus preached was, "Repent, for the kingdom of heaven is at hand" (Matthew 4:17b). Matthew's gospel contains more than fifty references to the kingdom of God or the kingdom of heaven (synonymous terms that I use interchangeably).

In the introduction, we defined the kingdom of God as his kingship and everything that his kingship involves, including his power, his authority, his domain, and his subjects. Jesus proclaimed the good news about the kingdom of God, as Matthew wrote,

> Jesus was going throughout all Galilee, teaching in their synagogues and proclaiming the gospel of the kingdom, and healing every kind of disease and every kind of sickness among the people [Matthew 4:23].

What was the good news about the kingdom that Jesus was proclaiming? We can summarize it as follows:

- God has an eternal kingdom that encompasses the entire universe.
- That kingdom would soon make a dramatic new entrance upon the earth.
- There is a place and a role in it for everyone who will meet God's terms.

To better appreciate Jesus' kingdom credentials, we will consider six essential facts about his relationship to the kingdom of God.

1) He dwelled in heaven with the Father from before creation.
2) He came to earth from heaven in the incarnation.
3) He knew that at his ascension he would return to his position in heaven.
4) He knew that the Father would then put everything under his authority.
5) He is now in heaven at the right hand of the Father.
6) He has been given authority over everything in the kingdom of God.

6-3

HE DWELLED IN HEAVEN WITH THE FATHER FROM BEFORE CREATION

The beginning of the book of John uniquely refers to Jesus as "the Word."

> In the beginning was the Word, and the Word was with God, and the Word was God. He was in the beginning with God. All things came into being through Him, and apart from Him nothing came into being that has come into being [John 1:1–3].

Jesus, the Word, existed in the beginning with the Father and participated in creation.

> Yet for us there is but one God, the Father, from whom are all things and we exist for Him; and one Lord, Jesus Christ, by whom are all things, and we exist through Him [1 Corinthians 8:6].

6-4

HE CAME TO EARTH FROM HEAVEN IN THE INCARNATION

Jesus has knowledge about the Heavenly Father that no one else has. The Old Testament prophets faithfully proclaimed the information that God revealed to them about himself, but none of them had complete knowledge or understanding of him. Jesus, on the other hand, has complete knowledge and understanding of the Father because he has been with the Father from the beginning. Jesus voluntarily set aside his heavenly privileges and his glory and came to earth as a man in the incarnation. He often referred to himself as "the Son of Man," which was a way of saying that he was the Son of God, born into mankind.

Jesus confirmed on a number of occasions that he had come from heaven.

> "No one has ascended into heaven, but He who descended from heaven: the Son of Man" [John 3:13].

> "For I have come down from heaven, not to do My own will, but the will of Him who sent Me" [John 6:38].

> Jesus said to them, "If God were your Father, you would love Me, for I proceeded forth and have come from God, for I have not even come on My own initiative, but He sent Me" [John 8:42].

6-5

HE KNEW THAT AT HIS ASCENSION HE WOULD RETURN TO HIS POSITION IN HEAVEN

Jesus understood that when his earthly mission was complete, he would return to his position in heaven. Early in his ministry he asked his disciples,

> What then if you see the Son of Man ascending to where He was before? [John 6:62].

Describing events that occurred during the Last Supper, John wrote,

Jesus, knowing that the Father had given all things into His hands, and that He had come forth from God and was going back to God...[John 13:3].

Later during the Last Supper, Jesus declared,

I came forth from the Father and have come into the world; I am leaving the world again and going to the Father [John 16:28].

Then Jesus prayed,

Now, Father, glorify Me together with Yourself, with the glory which I had with You before the world was [John 17:5].

Early on the first Easter morning, Jesus requested of Mary Magdalene,

Stop clinging to Me, for I have not yet ascended to the Father; but go to My brethren and say to them, "I ascend to My Father and your Father, and My God and your God" [John 20:17].

At his ascension forty days later, Jesus returned to his place in heaven.

And after He had said these things, He was lifted up while they were looking on, and a cloud received Him out of their sight. And as they were gazing intently into the sky while He was going, behold, two men in white clothing stood beside them. They also said, "Men of Galilee, why do you stand looking into the sky? This Jesus, who has been taken up from you into heaven, will come in just the same way as you have watched Him go into heaven" [Acts 1:9–11].

6-6

HE KNEW THAT THE FATHER WOULD THEN PUT EVERYTHING UNDER HIS AUTHORITY

Psalm 110 is the beginning of an important scriptural thread about this matter of Jesus' authority.

The Lord says to my Lord: "Sit at My right hand until I make Your enemies a footstool for Your feet" [Psalm 110:1].

Jesus quoted that verse when he challenged some of the Pharisees' erroneous conclusions about the Messiah.

Now while the Pharisees were gathered together, Jesus asked them a question: "What do you think about the Christ, whose son is He?" They said to Him, "The son of David." He said to them, "Then how does David in the Spirit call Him 'Lord,' saying,

'The Lord said to my Lord, "Sit at My right hand, until I put Your enemies beneath Your feet"'?

"If David then calls Him 'Lord,' how is He his son?" No one was able to answer Him a word, nor did anyone dare from that day on to ask Him another question [Matthew 22:41–46].

A second important scriptural thread began with Daniel's vision of the authority that the Messiah would be given.

I kept looking in the night visions, and behold, with the clouds of heaven One like a Son of Man was coming, and He came up to the Ancient of Days and was presented before Him. And to Him was given dominion, glory and a kingdom, that all the peoples, nations and men of every language might serve Him. His dominion is an everlasting dominion which will not pass away; and His kingdom is one which will not be destroyed [Daniel 7:13–14].

During his trial before the Sanhedrin, Jesus merged those two threads, revealing that both Psalm 110:1 and Daniel 7:13–14 were speaking about him.

But He kept silent and did not answer. Again the high priest was questioning Him, and saying to Him, "Are You the Christ, the Son of the Blessed One?" And Jesus said, "I am; and you shall see the Son of Man sitting at the right hand of Power, and coming with the clouds of heaven" [Mark 14:61–62].

On two other occasions Jesus verified that the Father would put all things under his authority.

The Father loves the Son and has given all things into His hand [John 3:35].

All things have been handed over to Me by My Father [Matthew 11:27a].

6-7

HE IS NOW IN HEAVEN AT THE RIGHT HAND OF THE FATHER

M ark's gospel described Jesus' ascension as follows:

So then, when the Lord Jesus had spoken to them, He was received up into heaven and sat down at the right hand of God [Mark 16:19].

Peter added to the scripture thread that began in Psalm 110:1. He quoted it in his sermon on the day of Pentecost to proclaim that Jesus is at the right hand of the Father:

This Jesus God raised up again, to which we are all witnesses. Therefore having been exalted to the right hand of God, and having received from the Father the promise of the Holy Spirit, He has poured forth this which you both see and hear. For it was not David who ascended into heaven, but he himself says:

"The Lord said to my Lord, 'Sit at My right hand, until I make Your enemies a footstool for Your feet.'"

Therefore let all the house of Israel know for certain that God has made Him both Lord and Christ—this Jesus whom you crucified [Acts 2:32–36].

As he was being martyred, Stephen was allowed to look into heaven. He saw Jesus at God's right hand.

But being full of the Holy Spirit, he [Stephen] gazed intently into heaven and saw the glory of God, and Jesus standing at the right hand of God; and he said, "Behold, I see the heavens opened up and the Son of Man standing at the right hand of God" [Acts 7:55–56].

Hebrews 1:3b–4 corroborated that Jesus is now at God's right hand.

> When He had made purification of sins, He sat down at the right hand
> of the Majesty on high, having become as much better than the angels,
> as He has inherited a more excellent name than they.

Hebrews 1:13 also referred to the scripture thread that began in Psalm 110:1.

> But to which of the angels has He ever said,
> "Sit at My right hand, until I make Your enemies a footstool for Your feet"?

Hebrews 10:12–13 contains another reference to Psalm 110:1.

> But He, having offered one sacrifice for sins for all time, sat down at the
> right hand of God, waiting from that time onward until His enemies be
> made a footstool for His feet.

Jesus is at God's right hand.

6-8

HE HAS BEEN GIVEN AUTHORITY OVER EVERYTHING IN THE KINGDOM OF GOD

Just before he ascended, Jesus announced to everyone assembled there,

> All authority has been given to Me in heaven and on earth [Matthew
> 28:18b].

You have probably not thought much about it, but it required more supernatural power than any of us can conceive of for God to seat Jesus at his right hand and put everything under his authority. The reason that there was such a ferocious battle is that there was extremely powerful opposition. Satan and all his forces were mobilized to prevent it from happening. Paul described the event this way:

I pray that the eyes of your heart may be enlightened, so that you will know what is the hope of His calling, what are the riches of the glory of His inheritance in the saints, and what is the surpassing greatness of His power toward us who believe. These are in accordance with the working of the strength of His might which He brought about in Christ, when He raised Him from the dead and seated Him at His right hand in the heavenly places, far above all rule and authority and power and dominion, and every name that is named, not only in this age but also in the one to come. And He put all things in subjection under His feet, and gave Him as head over all things to the church, which is His body, the fullness of Him who fills all in all [Ephesians 1:18–23].

For this reason also, God highly exalted Him, and bestowed on Him the name which is above every name, so that at the name of Jesus every knee will bow, of those who are in heaven and on earth and under the earth, and that every tongue will confess that Jesus Christ is Lord, to the glory of God the Father [Philippians 2:9–11].

6-9
SUMMARY

We have looked at six important reasons why Jesus was able to speak so authoritatively about the kingdom of God. The central point is that he was describing the kingdom over which he now reigns.

So just as the tares are gathered up and burned with fire, so shall it be at the end of the age. The Son of Man will send forth His angels, and they will gather out of **His kingdom** all stumbling blocks, and those who commit lawlessness, and will throw them into the furnace of fire; in that place there will be weeping and gnashing of teeth [Matthew 13:40–42, emphasis added].

In section 7 we will study what Jesus revealed from his firsthand knowledge of the kingdom of God.

Section 7

WHAT JESUS REVEALED ABOUT THE KINGDOM OF GOD

7-1

INTRODUCTION

Uuring his time on earth, Jesus provided us with a number of parables, stories, and prophecies to prepare us for enjoying life in God's kingdom during "this present age." "This present age" is the time period that began when Jesus ascended to heaven after his resurrection, and will end when he returns again.

In this section, we will explore:

1) The principles that govern God's kingdom
2) Our mission to spread the message of God's kingdom
3) Events that were prophesied for the early church
4) Conditions that were prophesied for believers of all times
5) How physical death is handled in God's kingdom
6) When and how Jesus will return
7) Rewards and punishments at the end of this age

7-2

THE PRINCIPLES THAT GOVERN GOD'S KINGDOM

The focus of Jesus' teaching ministry during his time on the earth was upon the kingdom of God, revealing and explaining the key principles by which it operates. He did that because the Father and he knew that, to the degree that we understand and adhere to those principles, our lives will be more fulfilled and enriched, and we will have a greater impact for good upon the people with whom we come into contact.

Instead of describing the kingdom of God directly, Jesus often used parables. Those stories about ordinary people and everyday events illustrate, by analogy, the points that Jesus wished to convey. Jesus began many of his parables by saying, "The kingdom of heaven may be compared to," or, "The kingdom of heaven is like." For example,

Jesus presented another parable to them, saying, "The kingdom of heaven may be compared to a man who sowed good seed in his field" [Matthew 13:24].

He spoke another parable to them, "The kingdom of heaven is like leaven, which a woman took and hid in three pecks of flour until it was all leavened" [Matthew 13:33].

Matthew wrote that Jesus spoke to the multitudes in parables, and that he did not speak to them without a parable (Matthew 13:34). For many years I wondered why he did that. Initially I supposed that it must be too difficult to describe the kingdom of God to people because we lack the basis for comprehending it, much like trying to explain music to someone who was born deaf or colors to someone who was born blind. But one day as I was reading Mark 4:34, which says that he was explaining everything privately to his disciples, I understood. Jesus does not intend that we fully comprehend what he is saying, apart from having a personal relationship with him. It is only as the Holy Spirit explains to us what he means, as he himself did for his disciples long ago, that we can fully understand.

THE KINGDOM OF GOD GROWS IN THE SOIL OF OUR HEARTS

Imagine the scene as Jesus told this parable for the first time two thousand years ago. Jesus had gone out of the house where he was staying and was sitting by the lake. Such large crowds gathered that he got into a little boat and sat in it while all the people stood on shore. Many of them probably stood with their feet in the water, trying to be as close as possible to Jesus. As he began to speak, a surprising hush fell over the eager crowd as they strained to hear every word.

And He spoke many things to them in parables, saying, "Behold, the sower went out to sow; and as he sowed, some seeds fell beside the road, and the birds came and ate them up. Others fell on the rocky places, where they did not have much soil; and immediately they sprang up, because they had no depth of soil. But when the sun had risen, they were scorched; and because they had no root, they withered away. Others fell among the thorns, and the thorns came up and choked them out. And others fell on the good soil and yielded a crop, some a hundredfold, some sixty, and some thirty. He who has ears, let him hear" [Matthew 13:3–9; see also Mark 4:3–9].

Jesus was an amazing teacher. His disciples and the crowd listened intently as he told that parable. They could envision the farmer sowing seed. They could visualize some of the seed being eaten by birds, some sprouting and wilting under the hot sun, some growing but later being crowded out by thorn bushes, and some ripening into a fine crop. However, they did not understand what the parable really meant. They did not perceive the spiritual analogy, the insights into the kingdom of God that Jesus was illustrating. Surely it meant more than that a farmer should be careful when he was sowing seed. Mark wrote,

> As soon as He was alone, His followers, along with the twelve, began asking Him about the parables. And He said to them, "Do you not understand this parable? How will you understand all the parables?" [Mark 4:10,13].

Then Jesus explained to them how the details of that parable represented truths about the kingdom of God. The parable about sowing seed is a prototype parable because his explanation of it provides a pattern for understanding other parables that he would tell.

> Hear then the parable of the sower. When anyone hears the word of the kingdom and does not understand it, the evil one comes and snatches away what has been sown in his heart. This is the one on whom seed was sown beside the road. The one on whom seed was sown on the rocky places, this is the man who hears the word and immediately receives it with joy; yet he has no firm root in himself, but is only temporary, and when affliction or persecution arises because of the word, immediately he falls away. And the one on whom seed was sown among the thorns, this is the man who hears the word, and the worry of the world and the deceitfulness of wealth choke the word, and it becomes unfruitful. And the one on whom seed was sown on the good soil, this is the man who hears the word and understands it; who indeed bears fruit and brings forth, some a hundredfold, some sixty, and some thirty [Matthew 13:18–23].

That parable, like many of Jesus' other parables, can have multiple applications. First, the parable shows the different ways that a group can respond to a message about the kingdom of God. A group's responses can be placed into one of four categories (soils):

1)   Some do not understand the message and dismiss it or quickly forget it (the soil beside the road).

2)   Some initially embrace the message but without much commitment (the shallow soil). They abandon the teachings when they are confronted with criticism or persecution for following them.

3)   Others embrace the message but later become side-tracked when they face conflicts between the teachings and their own goals and desires (thorny soil).

4)   Some wholeheartedly embrace the message and implement its teachings in their lives. Persisting through life's trials and difficulties, they remain faithful and focused. As a result, their lives bear much fruit for the kingdom of God (good soil).

Second, the parable shows how we as individuals react in different ways to different messages. The key is to remember that we each have all four types of soil within us. Because of that, our responses to different messages about the kingdom of God may differ greatly, depending on the subject matter of that message. For example, we might be good soil in response to a message to repent, but worry about our finances when we are challenged to give or to tithe. We might be shallow soil when asked to witness about Jesus and be totally unreceptive when asked to forgive someone.

The key question that each one of us must ask is this: "What do I need to do or change or forsake or implement so that I will be good soil for God's kingdom in every area of my life?" The first step in finding those answers is to acknowledge our responsibility to cooperate with God's plan for our lives. He needs our cooperation in order to transform our attitudes, thought patterns, prejudices, and negative reactions so that we become good soil in which his kingdom can flourish.

THE KINGDOM OF GOD IS LIKE A HIDDEN TREASURE

Jesus had a wonderful way of explaining the kingdom of God with examples that captured people's imaginations. A great example is how he compared the joy and excitement of finding hidden treasures to the joy and excitement of discovering life in the kingdom of God.

> The kingdom of heaven is like a treasure hidden in the field, which a man found and hid again; and from joy over it he goes and sells all that he has and buys that field [Matthew 13:44].

Whenever I read that verse, I usually imagine someone like Indiana Jones digging up an old treasure chest. When he opens it, he discovers that it is brimming with gold and silver coins. A contemporary example might be finding valuable minerals or a significant oil deposit beneath a field. Can you imagine how excited that would make you? Can't you envision your joy in selling everything you own and buying that field? That is the comparison Jesus was making in this parable.

The parable also provides further insight when we think about the field where the treasure is hidden. What is the field? The field is Jesus, as Paul wrote,

> Christ Himself, in whom are hidden all the treasures of wisdom and knowledge [Colossians 2:2c–3].

There are many who have had to make a choice between the spiritual treasure found in Christ or great treasure to enjoy on earth. Moses, as the adopted son of Pharaoh's daughter, was in line to inherit fabulous wealth and privileges. But the Bible says of Moses,

> By faith Moses, when he had grown up, refused to be called the son of Pharaoh's daughter, choosing rather to endure ill-treatment with the people of God than to enjoy the passing pleasures of sin, considering the reproach of Christ greater riches than the treasures of Egypt; for he was looking to the reward [Hebrews 11:24–26].

Moses discovered that field and gave up everything so he could acquire it. And wouldn't you agree that his decision paid off handsomely for him in ways that far exceeded anything he could have imagined? He became the liberator and the leader of Israel, became known as the friend of God, wrote the first five books of the Bible, and has for more than three thousand years been recognized as one of the world's great religious leaders.

Jesus is a treasure that is greatly to be desired.

> And coming to Him as to a living stone which has been rejected by men, but is choice and precious in the sight of God...For this is contained in Scripture:

"Behold, I lay in Zion a choice stone, a precious corner stone,
And he who believes in Him will not be disappointed."
This precious value, then, is for you who believe; [1 Peter 2:4,6–7a].

Once we envision Jesus as he is now, in all his glory, magnificence, radiance, love, mercy, joy, power, dominion, and authority, we will appreciate how much more valuable he is than anything else we could ever have. It then becomes much easier to abandon whatever might be preventing us from obtaining the promise of enjoying life forever with him in the kingdom of God.

In another parable, Jesus compared the kingdom of God to a merchant who buys and sells top quality pearls.

Again, the kingdom of heaven is like a merchant seeking fine pearls, and upon finding one pearl of great value, he went and sold all that he had and bought it [Matthew 13:45–46].

This parable is similar to the previous one from the standpoint of Jesus as the pearl of great value and us as the merchant who sells everything to acquire that pearl. Every successful merchant is able to appraise the items that he is considering buying. This particular merchant was a specialist in fine pearls. He would not buy one unless he believed he could resell it for enough profit to be worth his effort and risk. A purchase is an exceptional bargain when it is worth much more than its price. Jesus, the pearl of great value, is worth far more than we might have to pay, even if we spend everything that we have.

I mentioned earlier that Jesus' parables can have multiple applications. There is an important reciprocal application of this parable: To God, each of us is a pearl of great value. He purchased us with his most precious and valuable possession: the life of Jesus. There is a song that I love whose chorus begins,

You paid much too high a price for me,
Your tears, your blood, the pain,
To have my soul just stirred at times,
But never truly changed.

I remember sitting at my piano one day. I was feeling unimportant and of very little worth. I began singing that chorus: "You paid much too high a price for me." God immediately interrupted me. He spoke to my heart and said, "No, I did not!"

Startled, I asked, "What do you mean, Lord?"

Again he spoke to my heart and said, "I did not pay too high a price for you. I know what you are worth. I would have bankrupted all of heaven, if necessary, to redeem you."

I was astonished by what he said. I was also ashamed of having regarded myself as having so little value to God. But I am neither more valuable nor more special to God than you are. What he said to me that day, he says to you right now. "I know what you are worth. You are more precious to me than you could ever imagine. I would have bankrupted all of heaven, if necessary, to redeem you."

> Knowing that you were not redeemed with perishable things like silver or gold from your futile way of life inherited from your forefathers, but with precious blood, as of a lamb unblemished and spotless, the blood of Christ [1 Peter 1:18–19].

What great love God has for us. How valuable and precious we are in his sight. And oh, how much he wants us to be part of his kingdom, now and forever.

THE WHEAT AND THE TARES GROW TOGETHER IN GOD'S KINGDOM

This parable helps us to understand why there is evil in this world and God's ultimate plan for those who refuse to be a part of the kingdom of God. Jesus chose to use wheat and tares as metaphors for good and evil. Tares are weeds that resemble wheat when they are growing. Not only are they weeds, but if the plants become infected with a certain fungus, eating them can be fatal.

> Jesus presented another parable to them, saying, "The kingdom of heaven may be compared to a man who sowed good seed in his field. But while his men were sleeping, his enemy came and sowed tares among the wheat, and went away. But when the wheat sprouted and bore grain, then the tares became evident also. The slaves of the landowner came and said to him, 'Sir, did you not sow good seed in your field? How then does it have tares?' And he said to them, 'An enemy has done this!' The slaves said to him, 'Do you want us, then, to go and gather them up?' But he said, 'No; for while you are gathering up the tares, you may uproot

the wheat with them. Allow both to grow together until the harvest; and in the time of the harvest I will say to the reapers, "First gather up the tares and bind them in bundles to burn them up; but gather the wheat into my barn"" [Matthew 13:24–30].

The disciples asked Jesus to explain that parable.

And He said, "The one who sows the good seed is the Son of Man, and the field is the world; and as for the good seed, these are the sons of the kingdom; and the tares are the sons of the evil one; and the enemy who sowed them is the devil, and the harvest is the end of the age; and the reapers are angels. So just as the tares are gathered up and burned with fire, so shall it be at the end of the age. The Son of Man will send forth His angels, and they will gather out of His kingdom all stumbling blocks, and those who commit lawlessness, and will throw them into the furnace of fire; in that place there will be weeping and gnashing of teeth. Then the righteous will shine forth as the sun in the kingdom of their Father. He who has ears, let him hear" [Matthew 13:37–43].

Jesus' explanation provides insights into kingdom events that will occur at the end of the present age (which we will address in more detail later in this section). This parable acknowledges that there are children of the kingdom of God and children of the kingdom of Satan living together here on earth, and they look a lot alike. It confirms that God is fully aware of this, but he chooses to let it to be that way for now. There are at least two reasons for his doing so. First, he is allowing people as much time as possible to repent and turn to him.

The Lord is not slow about His promise, as some count slowness, but is patient toward you, not wishing for any to perish but for all to come to repentance [2 Peter 3:9].

Second, in his mercy to his own children, God has not suddenly removed all the members of Satan's kingdom. I intentionally wrote "in his mercy to his own children" because it would be deeply traumatic for us to lose those of our parents, grandparents, brothers, sisters, children, grandchildren, aunts, uncles, nieces, nephews, friends, neighbors, and acquaintances who are not yet citizens of God's kingdom. And that is what would happen if God suddenly removed everyone who is currently outside of his kingdom. Remember that before we were born again, we too were outside of God's kingdom. Where would we be now if God had suddenly "ripped out the tares" before we became citizens of his kingdom? In the same way that God was longsuffering and merciful with us, we want him to be patient and merciful with others. We want him to take as much time as he needs to bring as many people as possible into his kingdom.

Even though God has great patience, this parable illustrates that one day many who are not citizens of God's kingdom will be gathered up and "cast into the furnace of fire." Jesus was clearly revealing that there are only two ultimate destinations for each of us. We will either enjoy living forever with God in his kingdom or we will experience eternal death.

THE INJUSTICES OF LIFE ARE RECONCILED IN ETERNITY

Life can be unfair, but there is justice in eternity. Jesus told a story about a beggar named Lazarus and a rich man who died around the same time. Because of the many details such as the rich man's clothes, Lazarus lying at his gate, dogs licking Lazarus' sores, and the rich man having five brothers, I believe Jesus was relating an actual occurrence rather than telling a parable.

> Now there was a rich man, and he habitually dressed in purple and fine linen, joyously living in splendor every day. And a poor man named Lazarus was laid at his gate, covered with sores, and longing to be fed with the crumbs which were falling from the rich man's table; besides, even the dogs were coming and licking his sores [Luke 16:19–21].

Jesus did not say how the rich man became rich or how the poor man became poor. They were probably born into rich and poor families respectively. The poor man's plight had become even more difficult due to his medical problems. The story illustrates something that we all have observed: life can be unfair.

> Now the poor man died and was carried away by the angels to Abraham's bosom; and the rich man also died and was buried [Luke 16:22].

Regardless of what some people believe, physical death is not the end. We will exist forever. This parable affirms that when a righteous person dies, angels transport him to a place of comfort. In the Old Testament, that place was called Sheol; in the New Testament Greek it was called Hades. The Jews believed that Sheol (or Hades) was the home of both the righteous and the unrighteous dead, but it was separated into respective compartments. Abraham's bosom referred to the place of comfort where the righteous dead would reside until Judgment Day. The rich man, not being deemed righteous, was taken to an exceedingly unpleasant place that was also located in Sheol (or Hades).

> In Hades he lifted up his eyes, being in torment, and saw Abraham far away and Lazarus in his bosom. And he cried out and said, "Father Abraham, have mercy on me, and send Lazarus so that he may dip the tip of his finger in water and cool off my tongue, for I am in agony in this flame." But Abraham said, "Child, remember that during your life you received your good things, and likewise Lazarus bad things; but now he is being comforted here, and you are in agony" [Luke 16:23–25].

It is reassuring to learn that even though life is often unfair, the rewards and punishments in eternity will more than compensate for that. Abraham explained to the rich man that there was nothing he could do to change his situation at that point:

> "And besides all this, between us and you there is a great chasm fixed, so that those who wish to come over from here to you will not be able, and that none may cross over from there to us." And he [the rich man] said, "Then I beg you, father, that you send him to my father's house—for I have five brothers—in order that he may warn them, so that they will not also come to this place of torment." But Abraham said, "They have Moses and the Prophets; let them hear them." But he said, "No, father Abraham, but if someone goes to them from the dead, they will repent!" But he said to him, "If they do not listen to Moses and the Prophets, they will not be persuaded even if someone rises from the dead" [Luke 16:26–31].

One of our responsibilities as citizens of God's kingdom is to inform others about God, Jesus, the Holy Spirit, and the reality of God's kingdom. It is their responsibility to decide how much of what we share with them to believe and act upon.

MERCY AND GENEROSITY PREVAIL IN GOD'S KINGDOM

Life is not fair, but in eternity there is mercy and generosity. From a human standpoint, mercy and generosity can also seem unfair at times. Yet in the kingdom of heaven, there is a higher perspective. We can see this in Jesus' parable about the workers in the vineyard.

> For the kingdom of heaven is like a landowner who went out early in the morning to hire laborers for his vineyard. When he had agreed with the laborers for a denarius for the day, he sent them into his vineyard. And he went out about the third hour and saw others standing idle in the market place; and to those he said, "You also go into the vineyard, and whatever is right I will give you." And so they went. Again he went out about the sixth and the ninth hour, and did the same thing. And about the eleventh hour he went out and found others standing around; and he said to them, "Why have you been standing here idle all day long?" They said to him, "Because no one hired us." He said to them, "You go into the vineyard too."
>
> When evening came, the owner of the vineyard said to his foreman, "Call the laborers and pay them their wages, beginning with the last group to the first." When those hired about the eleventh hour came, each one received a denarius. When those hired first came, they thought that they would receive more; but each of them also received a denarius. When they received it, they grumbled at the landowner, saying, "These last men have worked only one hour, and you have made them equal to us who have borne the burden and the scorching heat of the day." But he answered and said to one of them, "Friend, I am doing you no wrong; did you not agree with me for a denarius? Take what is yours and go, but I wish to give to this last man the same as to you. Is it not lawful for me to do what I wish with what is my own? Or is your eye envious because I am generous?" So the last shall be first, and the first last [Matthew 20:1–16].

In that parable, the vineyard is the world, and God owns the vineyard. The laborers are the people who have responded to God's invitation to go to work for him. Everyone who agrees to do that will receive an identical reward—eternal life—regardless of how much or how little time they remain on the earth after accepting God's invitation. Another illustration of that is the account of the thief on the cross.

> One of the criminals who were hanged there was hurling abuse at Him, saying, "Are You not the Christ? Save Yourself and us!" But the other answered, and rebuking him said, "Do you not even fear God, since you are under the same sentence of condemnation? And we indeed are

suffering justly, for we are receiving what we deserve for our deeds; but this man has done nothing wrong." And he was saying, "Jesus, remember me when You come in Your kingdom!" And He said to him, "Truly I say to you, today you shall be with Me in Paradise" [Luke 23:39–43].

We receive the reward of eternal life in God's kingdom as soon as we accept his invitation to work for him. We will discuss other rewards later in this section.

Next let us look at some of the things Jesus revealed about life in the present age, which began with his ascension and will close when he returns to the earth.

7-3

OUR MISSION TO SPREAD THE MESSAGE OF GOD'S KINGDOM

Compared to the vastness of eternity, this present age is a tiny segment that began with Jesus' ascension to heaven about two thousand years ago. This age will end when Jesus returns to earth. The most important activity that will take place during this age is spreading the message of God's kingdom to those who have not heard it. For the duration of this present age, Jesus gave his disciples a clear message that he wanted them to share with the world.

> Then He opened their minds to understand the Scriptures, and He said to them, "Thus it is written, that the Christ would suffer and rise again from the dead the third day, and that repentance for forgiveness of sins would be proclaimed in His name to all the nations, beginning from Jerusalem. You are witnesses of these things" [Luke 24:45–48].

Jesus told them that their message was to be based upon the Scriptures. They were to tell people about his resurrection and his promise to forgive the sins of everyone who repents.

Forty days later, addressing those who had gathered to watch his ascension, Jesus issued the Great Commission.

> And Jesus came up and spoke to them, saying, "All authority has been given to Me in heaven and on earth. Go therefore and make disciples

of all the nations, baptizing them in the name of the Father and the Son and the Holy Spirit, teaching them to observe all that I commanded you; and lo, I am with you always, even to the end of the age" [Matthew 28:18–20].

Jesus began his message by affirming that God had entrusted him with full authority in heaven and on earth. Then he assigned them their mission: making disciples of people in every nation throughout the earth. It is the most important activity that will take place during this age. As part of their mission, they were to teach the new disciples to follow Jesus' directives. He promised they would not be operating on their own, but that he would be with them. Everyone who heard Jesus speak that day died long ago; hence, it is the responsibility of each new generation of kingdom citizens to continue working toward fulfilling that mission.

It is important to note that Jesus instructed them not to begin that mission until they had been equipped with the power of the Holy Spirit. The Holy Spirit's power in their lives would be essential to overcoming the obstacles, opposition, and persecution they would encounter.

And behold, I am sending forth the promise of My Father upon you; but you are to stay in the city until you are clothed with power from on high [Luke 24:49].

Gathering them together, He commanded them not to leave Jerusalem, but to wait for what the Father had promised, "Which," He said, "you heard of from Me; for John baptized with water, but you will be baptized with the Holy Spirit not many days from now" [Acts 1:4–5].

Incredibly, even after Jesus' explanations, the disciples were still expecting God's kingdom to be manifested by establishing Israel as a world power.

So when they had come together, they were asking Him, saying, "Lord, is it at this time You are restoring the kingdom to Israel?" He said to them, "It is not for you to know times or epochs which the Father has fixed by His own authority; but you will receive power when the Holy Spirit has come upon you; and you shall be My witnesses both in Jerusalem, and in all Judea and Samaria, and even to the remotest part of the earth" [Acts 1:6–8].

In response to their question about the kingdom of God, Jesus re-emphasized the necessity of being empowered by the Holy Spirit before they began their mission.

> And after He had said these things, He was lifted up while they were looking on, and a cloud received Him out of their sight [Acts 1:9].

It was at that time that the present age began. It will continue until Jesus returns to the earth.

7-4

HOW GOD'S KINGDOM GROWS

Jesus told two parables about seed to explain how the kingdom of God would spread during this age. The first one is about a mustard seed.

> He presented another parable to them, saying, "The kingdom of heaven is like a mustard seed, which a man took and sowed in his field; and this is smaller than all other seeds, but when it is full grown, it is larger than the garden plants and becomes a tree, so that the birds of the air come and nest in its branches" [Matthew 13:31–32].

A friend showed me some mustard seeds that he had brought back from Israel. I was surprised how different they were from the seeds we find in our deli mustard. They were hardly bigger than a particle of dust. The parable illustrates how the kingdom of God would grow and spread. Beginning with one hundred and twenty disciples on the day of Pentecost, it has grown for two millennia. It is now like a majestic tree in comparison to the size of a mustard seed. There are more than two billion citizens of the kingdom of God alive today, plus all those who are already in heaven.

This parable refuted the popular hope at the time that the kingdom of God would suddenly appear in Israel, rally large armies, militarily conquer the known world, and set up its capital in Jerusalem. That is not at all what the kingdom of God in this age is about.

In the second parable about how the kingdom of God would spread, the focus is on the crop.

And He was saying, "The kingdom of God is like a man who casts seed
upon the soil; and he goes to bed at night and gets up by day, and the
seed sprouts and grows—how, he himself does not know. The soil
produces crops by itself; first the blade, then the head, then the mature
grain in the head. But when the crop permits, he immediately puts in
the sickle, because the harvest has come" [Mark 4:26–29].

Like the man in this parable who sows seed, we must spread the word
about God's kingdom. But just as soil, water, and sunshine are what cause
seeds to grow, so God is the one who causes his kingdom to grow.

This parable hints that the kingdom may grow in identifiable stages,
with each stage transitioning naturally into the next. The parable implies
that the present age will continue until God determines that everything he
intends to accomplish has been accomplished. It is his goal to spread his
kingdom throughout the earth.

This gospel of the kingdom shall be preached in the whole world as
a testimony to all the nations, and then the end will come [Matthew
24:14].

In another parable, Jesus compared the spread of the kingdom to the
way leaven, or yeast, permeates flour and prepares it to be made into bread.

He spoke another parable to them, "The kingdom of heaven is like
leaven, which a woman took and hid in three pecks of flour until it was
all leavened" [Matthew 13:33].

One interpretation of this verse is that the flour represents us, and the
yeast represents the Holy Spirit as he dwells in us and prepares us to become
united with other citizens of the kingdom. 1 Corinthians 10:16b–17 likens
the body of Christ to a loaf of bread:

Is not the bread which we break a sharing in the body of Christ? Since
there is one bread, we who are many are one body; for we all partake of
the one bread.

Another interpretation is that the flour represents people in our
culture, and we are like the yeast whose purpose is to positively influence
and morally elevate society.

7-5

EVENTS PROPHESIED FOR THE EARLY CHURCH

Jesus foretold many future events and conditions that would occur. I am going to discuss these prophecies in two groups. The first group is the events which would impact the early disciples. The second group is the later events, which would be experienced by believers and the world in general. The early events occurred within the first one hundred and fifty years after Jesus' death. Jesus told his disciples about these events so that they would know how to respond. Here are three of the warnings that Jesus gave.

1) Persecution

First, Jesus wanted to prepare his disciples for the persecution they would face.

> But be on your guard; for they will deliver you to the courts, and you will be flogged in the synagogues, and you will stand before governors and kings for My sake, as a testimony to them [Mark 13:9].

He told them what to do when that happened.

> When they arrest you and hand you over, do not worry beforehand about what you are to say, but say whatever is given you in that hour; for it is not you who speak, but it is the Holy Spirit [Mark 13:11].

In other words, adversities can become opportunities for spreading the gospel. The book of Acts provides examples of that in the lives of Peter, John, and Paul.

2) Destruction of Jerusalem

Second, Jesus foretold coming national events, particularly the destruction of Jerusalem and the temple, which were the centerpieces of the Jewish religion. (This would be the second time Jerusalem was destroyed, the first being during the time of the prophet Jeremiah.)

> And while some were talking about the temple, that it was adorned with beautiful stones and votive gifts, He said, "As for these things which you are looking at, the days will come in which there will not be left one stone upon another which will not be torn down" [Luke 21:5–6].

Then Jesus told them how to identify when that devastation was imminent and what they must do.

> But when you see Jerusalem surrounded by armies, then recognize that her desolation is near. Then those who are in Judea must flee to the mountains, and those who are in the midst of the city must leave, and those who are in the country must not enter the city; because these are days of vengeance, so that all things which are written will be fulfilled. Woe to those who are pregnant and to those who are nursing babies in those days; for there will be great distress upon the land and wrath to this people; and they will fall by the edge of the sword, and will be led captive into all the nations; and Jerusalem will be trampled under foot by the Gentiles until the times of the Gentiles are fulfilled [Luke 21:20–24].

Jesus' prophecy was fulfilled beginning with the First Roman-Jewish War, also called the First Jewish Revolt (between A.D. 66 and A.D. 73). The sequence of events took place as Jesus had foretold. Following a lengthy siege by the Roman army, Jerusalem was captured and the temple was destroyed. The Second Roman-Jewish War, also called the Bar Kokhba Revolt, took place between A.D. 132 and A.D. 135. When Jerusalem fell that time, the Roman armies leveled the city, and the few Jews who survived were exiled.

3) SIGNS IN THE SUN, MOON, AND STARS

A third warning that Jesus gave his followers was that the appearance of the sun, moon, and stars would be affected.

> But immediately after the tribulation of those days the sun will be darkened, and the moon will not give its light, and the stars will fall from the sky, and the powers of the heavens will be shaken [Matthew 24:29].

I have heard sermons in which the speaker considered that verse to be literal rather than symbolic, and expected it to be fulfilled shortly before Jesus returns to the earth. There is an alternate interpretation that I believe better fits the context. To understand it, we have to look back to a dream that Joseph had about the sun, moon, and stars. His father Jacob interpreted the dream as applying to himself, his wife Rachel, and his other sons.

> Now he [Joseph] had still another dream, and related it to his brothers, and said, "Lo, I have had still another dream; and behold, the sun and the moon and eleven stars were bowing down to me." He related it to his father [Jacob] and to his brothers; and his father rebuked him and said to him, "What is this dream that you have had? Shall I and your mother and your brothers actually come to bow ourselves down before you to the ground?" [Genesis 37:9–10].

Joseph's dream was fulfilled after he rose to power in Egypt (see Genesis 43–45). Just as the sun, moon, and stars in Joseph's dream referred to people in positions of authority, I believe the sun, moon, and stars in Matthew 24:29 refer to the leadership of the Jewish nation. Therefore, this verse is not a reference to end-time events but to the devastation of the Jewish nation following the Roman-Jewish Wars.

7-6

CONDITIONS THAT WERE PROPHESIED FOR BELIEVERS OF ALL TIMES

In addition to warning his early followers of events they would experience, Jesus also gave information for his later followers about what they would experience. Jesus' prophecies can be grouped into three categories: 1) recurring events that would take place all over the world, 2) persecution that would be experienced, and 3) false christs that would arise multiple times.

1) WORLDWIDE EVENTS

Let's look first at how Jesus described events that would take place all over the world, such as recurring wars and frequent natural disasters.

> "When you hear of wars and disturbances, do not be terrified; for these things must take place first, but the end does not follow immediately."

> Then He continued by saying to them, "Nation will rise against nation
> and kingdom against kingdom, and there will be great earthquakes, and
> in various places plagues and famines; and there will be terrors and
> great signs from heaven" [Luke 21:9–11].

Events like those that Jesus mentioned are not unusual. Such events
affect large numbers of people regardless of whether or not they are citizens of the kingdom. Jesus told his followers not to be frightened each
time something like that happened. He also told them not to interpret such
events as signs that the end of the age was near.

2) PERSECUTION

Second, Jesus began as early as the Sermon on the Mount to warn his
followers that they would experience persecution. They could expect to be
despised and persecuted for two reasons: 1) for living moral lives and 2) for
believing in Jesus. He told them not to fear persecution. Instead they should
rejoice when it occurred because God would reward their endurance and
suffering.

> Blessed are those who have been persecuted for the sake of righteousness,
> for theirs is the kingdom of heaven. Blessed are you when people insult
> you and persecute you, and falsely say all kinds of evil against you
> because of Me. Rejoice and be glad, for your reward in heaven is great;
> for in the same way they persecuted the prophets who were before you
> [Matthew 5:10–12].

We must be careful, though, that whatever persecution we experience is
the result of our trying to live moral lives and follow Jesus, not because we
are displaying judgmental attitudes or offensive behavior.

Jesus said that some of his followers could even expect hostility from
members of their own families.

> Brother will betray brother to death, and a father his child; and children
> will rise up against parents and have them put to death. You will be
> hated by all because of My name, but the one who endures to the end,
> he will be saved [Mark 13:12–13].

During the Last Supper, Jesus also spoke about persecution.

If the world hates you, you know that it has hated Me before it hated you. If you were of the world, the world would love its own; but because you are not of the world, but I chose you out of the world, because of this the world hates you. Remember the word that I said to you, "A slave is not greater than his master." If they persecuted Me, they will also persecute you; if they kept My word, they will keep yours also. But all these things they will do to you for My name's sake, because they do not know the One who sent Me [John 15:18–21].

As Jesus' followers, we can expect to experience similar treatment. But let's not deliberately precipitate it by being antagonistic and judgmental toward those who are not yet in God's kingdom.

3) FALSE PROPHETS

The third warning Jesus gave was about false prophets who would claim to be the Christ. Jesus warned us not to be misled into thinking that he would make a secret return prior to the close of the age.

Then if anyone says to you, "Behold, here is the Christ," or "There He is," do not believe him. For false Christs and false prophets will arise and will show great signs and wonders, so as to mislead, if possible, even the elect. Behold, I have told you in advance. So if they say to you, "Behold, He is in the wilderness," do not go out, or, "Behold, He is in the inner rooms," do not believe them [Matthew 24:23–26].

7-7

PHYSICAL DEATH: THE DOORWAY TO ETERNITY

B ecause we have been addressing how to live in the kingdom of God here and now, it is necessary for us to look at an event that each one of us will experience: the day when our earthly lives end. That day will come in one of two ways: either we will die physically or Jesus will return to the earth. Let's look first at physical death and how Jesus prepared his followers for it. After that, we will look at what the Bible says about Jesus' return.

Physical death is the norm for people. Only two individuals in biblical history evaded it: Enoch and Elijah. In both of those cases, God sovereignly took them to heaven while they were still alive.

> By faith Enoch was taken up so that he would not see death; and he was not found because God took him up; for he obtained the witness that before his being taken up he was pleasing to God [Hebrews 11:5].

> As they [Elijah and Elisha] were going along and talking, behold, there appeared a chariot of fire and horses of fire which separated the two of them. And Elijah went up by a whirlwind to heaven [2 Kings 2:11].

Everyone else in the Bible, including Jesus, experienced physical death.

There were a few people in the Bible who actually experienced physical death twice because they were raised from the dead.

- The son of the Shunammite woman was raised to life by Elisha (2 Kings 4:18–36).
- Jesus called Lazarus back to life (John 11:1–45).
- Jesus also raised the son of the widow of Nain from the dead (Luke 7:11–15).
- Peter raised Tabitha (Acts 9:36–41).
- It is possible that Paul died and returned to life after being stoned by a mob (Acts 14:19–20).
- Paul raised a young man from the dead (Acts 20:9–10).

Still today there are accounts of people being miraculously raised from the dead. Even so, when someone is raised from the dead, it is temporary. Eventually they will die again. Since it is likely we will each die, it would be a source of comfort to know what to expect when that happens. Let's see what we can learn from the biblical account of Jesus raising Lazarus from the dead.

Mary and Martha sent a message to Jesus that their brother Lazarus was sick, but by the time Jesus reached their home, Lazarus had already died. Martha expressed deep disappointment that Jesus had not arrived in time to heal her brother.

> Martha then said to Jesus, "Lord, if You had been here, my brother would not have died. Even now I know that whatever You ask of God, God will give You." Jesus said to her, "Your brother will rise again." Martha said to Him, "I know that he will rise again in the resurrection on the last day." Jesus said to her, "I am the resurrection and the life; he who believes in

Me will live even if he dies, and everyone who lives and believes in Me will never die. Do you believe this?" [John 11:21–26].

What did Jesus mean when he said that everyone who believes in him will never die? He certainly could not have been promising that we would not die physically. What he meant was that even though our bodies may die, the real part of us will not die. We are eternal beings.

Jesus said,

This is eternal life, that they may know You, the only true God, and Jesus Christ whom You have sent [John 17:3].

One of the things that will happen in heaven is that we will get to know Jesus and the Father in more profound and intimate ways. However, I have some wonderful news. We don't have to wait until we die to begin to get to know Jesus and the Father better. We can be doing that here and now. It is one of our greatest privileges as citizens of God's kingdom. But even so, an entirely new relationship with Jesus and the Father will open up to us in heaven.

What else will we experience during eternal life? During the Last Supper, Jesus revealed to his disciples,

In My Father's house are many dwelling places; if it were not so, I would have told you; for I go to prepare a place for you [John 14:2].

Based on what Jesus disclosed, we can expect to have our own dwelling places in heaven. Even better, Jesus said he will be there with us.

If I go and prepare a place for you, I will come again and receive you to Myself, that where I am, there you may be also [John 14:3].

It is Jesus' desire that we be with him for eternity:

Father, I desire that they also, whom You have given Me, be with Me where I am, so that they may see My glory...[John 17:24a].

Isn't it marvelous that our heavenly dwelling places will be so close to Jesus!

So far we've talked about having houses in heaven and being with Jesus, but we haven't talked about how we will get to heaven after we die. In relating the account of the rich man and Lazarus (not Martha's brother but a different Lazarus), Jesus said,

> Now the poor man died and was carried away by the angels to Abraham's bosom; and the rich man also died and was buried [Luke 16:22].

Like Lazarus, when we die, angels will transport us to heaven. According to what Jesus told the thief on the cross as he was dying, there is no delay before we enter heaven.

> Truly I say to you, today you shall be with Me in Paradise [Luke 23:43].

Jesus told him "today." We, like the thief on the cross, will be transported to heaven as soon as we die. We will not spend some period of time in an intermediate place. There is no mention in the Bible of a concept such as purgatory.

God sometimes gives individuals surprising glimpses or previews of what heaven is like. Paul wrote about such an experience that he had.

> I will go on to visions and revelations of the Lord. I know a man in Christ who fourteen years ago—whether in the body I do not know, or out of the body I do not know, God knows—such a man was caught up to the third heaven. And I know how such a man—whether in the body or apart from the body I do not know, God knows—was caught up into Paradise and heard inexpressible words, which a man is not permitted to speak [2 Corinthians 12:1b–4].

After that experience, Paul had a deep longing to return to heaven. He wrote that he was eager to be with Jesus.

> Therefore, being always of good courage, and knowing that while we are at home in the body we are absent from the Lord—for we walk by faith, not by sight—we are of good courage, I say, and prefer rather to be absent from the body and to be at home with the Lord [2 Corinthians 5:6–8].

> For to me, to live is Christ and to die is gain. But if I am to live on in the flesh, this will mean fruitful labor for me; and I do not know which to choose. But I am hard-pressed from both directions, having the desire to depart and be with Christ, for that is very much better [Philippians 1:21–23].

Physical death for citizens of God's kingdom is not something to be feared. It is merely the doorway through which we enter heaven. We can be confident that everything God has for us there will be exceedingly more wonderful than we could imagine on our own.

But just as it is written,

"Things which eye has not seen and ear has not heard,
And which have not entered the heart of man,
All that God has prepared for those who love Him."

For to us God revealed them through the Spirit; for the Spirit searches all things, even the depths of God [1 Corinthians 2:9–10].

7-8

WHEN WILL JESUS RETURN?

This present age will come to a close when Jesus returns to earth. Those who are alive at that time will not experience physical death. In what manner will Jesus return? According to the angels who were present when Jesus ascended from earth to heaven, he would return in the same way that he left.

And after He [Jesus] had said these things, He was lifted up while they were looking on, and a cloud received Him out of their sight. And as they were gazing intently into the sky while He was going, behold, two men in white clothing stood beside them. They also said, "Men of Galilee, why do you stand looking into the sky? This Jesus, who has been taken up from you into heaven, will come in just the same way as you have watched Him go into heaven" [Acts 1:9–11].

Jesus' disciples asked him what sign would precede the end of the age.

As He was sitting on the Mount of Olives, the disciples came to Him privately, saying, "Tell us, when will these things [the destruction of the temple] happen, and what will be the sign of Your coming, and of the end of the age?" [Matthew 24:3].

Jesus told them when the end of the age would come in Matthew 24:14.

> This gospel of the kingdom shall be preached in the whole world as a
> testimony to all the nations, and then the end will come.

This age will continue until the gospel has been successfully preached
throughout the entire world, something that has not yet been fulfilled.
Notice that Jesus did not say that the age would then immediately end. This
age will continue for as long as God wants it to. It will continue until he
accomplishes everything that he intends to accomplish during it.

Another part of the disciples' question in Matthew 24:3 concerned
events which would indicate his return was imminent. Jesus' reply was that
the timing of his return cannot be predicted. Only the Father knows when
his return will be.

> But of that day and hour no one knows, not even the angels of heaven,
> nor the Son, but the Father alone [Matthew 24:36].

Furthermore, there will not be any specific signs or events to indicate
his return is imminent. Just prior to his return, everything will seem to be
normal.

> And just as it happened in the days of Noah, so it will be also in the
> days of the Son of Man: they were eating, they were drinking, they were
> marrying, they were being given in marriage, until the day that Noah
> entered the ark, and the flood came and destroyed them all. It was
> the same as happened in the days of Lot: they were eating, they were
> drinking, they were buying, they were selling, they were planting, they
> were building; but on the day that Lot went out from Sodom it rained
> fire and brimstone from heaven and destroyed them all. It will be just
> the same on the day that the Son of Man is revealed [Luke 17:26–30].

On two other occasions Jesus affirmed that the timing of his return
cannot be predicted.

> For the Son of Man is coming at an hour when you do not think He will
> [Matthew 24:44b].

> Be on the alert then, for you do not know the day nor the hour [Matthew
> 25:13].

Paul also wrote that the timing of Jesus' return cannot be forecast.

Now as to the times and the epochs, brethren, you have no need of anything to be written to you. For you yourselves know full well that the day of the Lord will come just like a thief in the night. While they are saying, "Peace and safety!" then destruction will come upon them suddenly like labor pains upon a woman with child, and they will not escape [1 Thessalonians 5:1–3].

We will all be taken by surprise when Jesus returns. I laughed at a sign I saw in a church office that read, "Jesus is coming soon—everybody try to look busy!" But we do not need to agonize about when Jesus might return.

But you, brethren, are not in darkness, that the day would overtake you like a thief; for you are all sons of light and sons of day. We are not of night nor of darkness; so then let us not sleep as others do, but let us be alert and sober [1 Thessalonians 5:4–6].

In the light of what we have studied about the kingdom of God, what should we do as we await Jesus' return? Jesus told a parable to illustrate that for us.

Take heed, keep on the alert; for you do not know when the appointed time will come. It is like a man away on a journey, who upon leaving his house and putting his slaves in charge, assigning to each one his task, also commanded the doorkeeper to stay on the alert. Therefore, be on the alert—for you do not know when the master of the house is coming, whether in the evening, at midnight, or when the rooster crows, or in the morning—in case he should come suddenly and find you asleep. What I say to you I say to all, "Be on the alert!" [Mark 13:33–37].

In that parable, Jesus is the man who went on a journey of undefined duration. We are the servants to whom he has given assignments. None of us knows when our appointed times will be. It may be when Jesus returns at the end of the age, but more likely it will be when we die physically. Either of those events can occur suddenly and without warning. In the meantime, our task is to work faithfully and diligently on our assignments from the Lord, whatever they may be.

7-9

THE SEQUENCE OF EVENTS THAT PRECEDE JESUS' RETURN

If we look more deeply into what the Bible says about Jesus' return to the earth, our expectation may start to differ slightly from the most popular one. Instead of expecting a single instantaneous event, it makes more sense to visualize his return as a sequence of events that unfolds over a period of days, weeks, or perhaps even longer.

Here is a brief summary of the main activities. They will begin with dramatic signs in the heavens. The righteous dead will be resurrected. Angels will bring the citizens of God's kingdom who are alive on the earth to join them. The angels will then remove from the earth those non-citizens who are deemed to be incorrigibly evil. The remainder of the non-citizens who are living on earth will be assembled there. Jesus will ascend to his throne. He will judge everyone, assigning appropriate rewards or punishments to each person. Let's now consider each of those events in greater detail.

SIGNS IN THE HEAVENS

Jesus' return will be spectacular. It will be heralded by astonishing signs in the sky that will be impossible for anyone to miss. Describing this, Jesus said,

> For just like the lightning, when it flashes out of one part of the sky, shines to the other part of the sky, so will the Son of Man be in His day [Luke 17:24].

Everyone who has chosen to live apart from God's grace and mercy will realize that they are in serious trouble.

> And then the sign of the Son of Man will appear in the sky, and then all the tribes of the earth will mourn, and they will see the Son of Man coming on the clouds of the sky with power and great glory [Matthew 24:30].

On the other hand, everyone who has been looking forward to his return will rejoice.

> But when these things begin to take place, straighten up and lift up your heads, because your redemption is drawing near [Luke 21:28].

THE FAITHFUL ASSEMBLED

Angels will gather the citizens of God's kingdom, those who are alive on earth as well as those who have died.

> And then He will send forth the angels, and will gather together His elect from the four winds, from the farthest end of the earth to the farthest end of heaven [Mark 13:27].

> I tell you, on that night there will be two in one bed; one will be taken and the other will be left. There will be two women grinding at the same place; one will be taken and the other will be left. Two men will be in the field; one will be taken and the other will be left [Luke 17:34–36].

It is interesting that Luke's narrative hints at an understanding that the earth is round. People in various places around the earth will be engaged in activities appropriate to their time of the day.

RESURRECTION

Although other people in the Bible had been temporarily raised to life, Jesus was the first to be truly resurrected. The significance of his resurrection is that it proves the reality of resurrection and thereby provides hope for us. When Jesus returns, every citizen of God's kingdom who has died will be resurrected just as Jesus was.

> But now Christ has been raised from the dead, the first fruits of those who are asleep. For since by a man came death, by a man also came the resurrection of the dead. For as in Adam all die, so also in Christ all will be made alive. But each in his own order: Christ the first fruits, after that those who are Christ's at His coming [1 Corinthians 15:20–23].

It will not be necessary to resurrect the citizens of the kingdom who are living on earth when Jesus returns. Instead, they will be given their immortal bodies at that time. Paul described this to the church in Corinth.

> Behold, I tell you a mystery; we will not all sleep, but we will all be changed, in a moment, in the twinkling of an eye, at the last trumpet; for the trumpet will sound, and the dead will be raised imperishable, and we will be changed. For this perishable must put on the imperishable, and this mortal must put on immortality. But when this perishable will have put on the imperishable, and this mortal will have put on immortality, then will come about the saying that is written, "Death is swallowed up in victory" [1 Corinthians 15:51–54].

Paul also described it to the church in Thessalonica.

> But we do not want you to be uninformed, brethren, about those who are asleep, so that you will not grieve as do the rest who have no hope. For if we believe that Jesus died and rose again, even so God will bring with Him those who have fallen asleep in Jesus. For this we say to you by the word of the Lord, that we who are alive and remain until the coming of the Lord, will not precede those who have fallen asleep. For the Lord Himself will descend from heaven with a shout, with the voice of the archangel and with the trumpet of God, and the dead in Christ will rise first. Then we who are alive and remain will be caught up together with them in the clouds to meet the Lord in the air, and so we shall always be with the Lord. Therefore comfort one another with these words [1 Thessalonians 4:13–18].

In answer to the intriguing question of what our immortal bodies will be like, Paul described them as being the same kind of body that Jesus has.

> The first man [Adam] is from the earth, earthy; the second man [Jesus] is from heaven. As is the earthy, so also are those who are earthy; and as is the heavenly, so also are those who are heavenly. Just as we have borne the image of the earthy, we will also bear the image of the heavenly [1 Corinthians 15:47–49].

> For our citizenship is in heaven, from which also we eagerly wait for a Savior, the Lord Jesus Christ; who will transform the body of our humble state into conformity with the body of His glory, by the exertion of the power that He has even to subject all things to Himself [Philippians 3:20–21].

Since our immortal bodies will "bear the image of the heavenly," like Jesus' immortal body, let's look again at the biblical account of Jesus' resurrection so we can learn more about what will happen.

Jesus told his disciples how certain prophecies in the Old Testament foretold that he would be killed and then be resurrected on the third day.

> Then He took the twelve aside and said to them, "Behold, we are going up to Jerusalem, and all things which are written through the prophets about the Son of Man will be accomplished. For He will be handed over to the Gentiles, and will be mocked and mistreated and spit upon, and after they have scourged Him, they will kill Him; and the third day He will rise again" [Luke 18:31–33].

On that first Good Friday, Jesus died by crucifixion.

> When they came to the place called The Skull, there they crucified Him and the criminals, one on the right and the other on the left [Luke 23:33].

> And Jesus, crying out with a loud voice, said, "Father, into Your hands I commit My spirit." Having said this, He breathed His last [Luke 23:46].

> This man [Joseph of Arimathea] went to Pilate and asked for the body of Jesus. And he took it down and wrapped it in a linen cloth, and laid Him in a tomb cut into the rock, where no one had ever lain [Luke 23:52–53].

Our body, like Jesus' body, may one day die. When Jesus sensed that his physical death was at hand, he committed his spirit to God. Our spirit, like his, will never die but will live forever.

By the third day after his death (the first Easter morning), Jesus had risen from the dead. Several women came to the tomb to embalm his body, and they were addressed by angels who were at the tomb:

> Why do you seek the living One among the dead? He is not here, but He has risen. Remember how He spoke to you while He was still in Galilee, saying that the Son of Man must be delivered into the hands of sinful men, and be crucified, and the third day rise again [Luke 24:5b–7].

That evening Jesus appeared unexpectedly to his disciples in his resurrected body. Apparently he did not look exactly as they remembered him.

He Himself stood in their midst. But they were startled and frightened and thought that they were seeing a spirit. And He said to them, "Why are you troubled, and why do doubts arise in your hearts? See My hands and My feet, that it is I Myself; touch Me and see, for a spirit does not have flesh and bones as you see that I have." And when He had said this, He showed them His hands and His feet. While they still could not believe it because of their joy and amazement, He said to them, "Have you anything here to eat?" They gave Him a piece of a broiled fish; and He took it and ate it before them [Luke 24:36b, 37–43].

Those verses confirm that the resurrected Jesus was not in the form of a disembodied spirit. He had a body that enabled him to function in the physical world. His resurrection body looked similar to and had many of the same features as his previous earthly body. He had arms and hands, legs and feet. His hands, feet, and side retained the wounds he had suffered during his crucifixion, although the wounds from the beating and from the crown of thorns seem to have disappeared. He could see and hear, speak, move about, and eat. The most unusual feature about his resurrected body was that he could appear and disappear at will. The reality of Jesus' death and resurrection is at the heart of the gospel message.

For I delivered to you as of first importance what I also received, that Christ died for our sins according to the Scriptures, and that He was buried, and that He was raised on the third day according to the Scriptures, and that He appeared to Cephas [Peter], then to the twelve. After that He appeared to more than five hundred brethren at one time [1 Corinthians 15:3–6a].

We can rejoice as we look forward expectantly to the day of Jesus' return to the earth.

7-10

REWARDS AND PUNISHMENTS UPON JESUS' RETURN

Upon Jesus' return to earth, rewards and punishments will be given to three categories of people:

1) The righteous dead who have now been resurrected
2) The citizens of God's kingdom who are alive at his return and have now been given immortal bodies
3) Everyone else who is alive when he returns (those who are incorrigibly wicked and those who are *not* incorrigibly wicked).

We need to look at several teachings of Jesus to get the full picture of what will happen to these groups. The first teaching we will examine uses a fishing metaphor to explain what will happen to those on earth who are incorrigibly wicked when Jesus returns.

> Again, the kingdom of heaven is like a dragnet cast into the sea, and gathering fish of every kind; and when it was filled, they drew it up on the beach; and they sat down and gathered the good fish into containers, but the bad they threw away. So it will be at the end of the age; the angels shall come forth and take out the wicked from among the righteous, and will throw them into the furnace of fire; in that place there shall be weeping and gnashing of teeth [Matthew 13:47–50].

Angels will separate the wicked from the righteous and take them to join the unrighteous dead. Most people assume that the weeping and gnashing of teeth mentioned in those verses are caused by the discomfort of the heat and flames. That is certainly true. But there may be another important factor that is involved as well. It may be that God will at that time reveal to each person the kind of life God had planned for them to live. Some of their weeping and gnashing of teeth may be because people now realize the wonderful blessings, relationships, and experiences they forfeited by choosing to live apart from God.

While the punishment for those who are evil might seem harsh, Jesus made it clear that all people have the opportunity to be a part of God's kingdom, regardless of their level of ability or talent. He explained this with a parable about slaves whose master gave each of them an equal portion of money to use for business while he was traveling. The story not only demonstrates how faith and hope are rewarded but also how disobedience is punished.

> While they were listening to these things, Jesus went on to tell a parable, because He was near Jerusalem, and they supposed that the kingdom of God was going to appear immediately. So He said, "A nobleman went

to a distant country to receive a kingdom for himself, and then return.
And he called ten of his slaves, and gave them ten minas and said to
them, 'Do business with this until I come back.' But his citizens hated
him and sent a delegation after him, saying, 'We do not want this man
to reign over us.'

When he returned, after receiving the kingdom, he ordered that these
slaves, to whom he had given the money, be called to him so that he
might know what business they had done.

The first appeared, saying, 'Master, your mina has made ten minas
more.' And he said to him, 'Well done, good slave, because you have
been faithful in a very little thing, you are to be in authority over ten
cities.'

The second came, saying, 'Your mina, master, has made five minas.' And
he said to him also, 'And you are to be over five cities.'

Another came, saying, 'Master, here is your mina, which I kept put away
in a handkerchief; for I was afraid of you, because you are an exacting
man; you take up what you did not lay down and reap what you did not
sow.'

He said to him, 'By your own words I will judge you, you worthless slave.
Did you know that I am an exacting man, taking up what I did not lay
down and reaping what I did not sow? Then why did you not put my
money in the bank, and having come, I would have collected it with
interest?'

Then he said to the bystanders, 'Take the mina away from him and give
it to the one who has the ten minas.' And they said to him, 'Master, he
has ten minas already.'

I tell you that to everyone who has, more shall be given, but from the
one who does not have, even what he does have shall be taken away. But
these enemies of mine, who did not want me to reign over them, bring
them here and slay them in my presence" [Luke 19:11–27].

One of the main points of that parable is to assure us that when
Jesus returns, he will give rewards to everyone who faithfully did as he
directed them. And those rewards will far surpass the value of people's
accomplishments.

Therefore, my beloved brethren, be steadfast, immovable, always abounding in the work of the Lord, knowing that your toil is not in vain in the Lord [1 Corinthians 15:58].

For we must all appear before the judgment seat of Christ, so that each one may be recompensed for his deeds in the body, according to what he has done, whether good or bad [2 Corinthians 5:10].

We will also be rewarded for faithfulness and for acts of righteousness, kindness, and generosity. We will receive some of those rewards during our lifetimes. We will receive the rest after Jesus returns.

So when you give to the poor, do not sound a trumpet before you, as the hypocrites do in the synagogues and in the streets, so that they may be honored by men. Truly I say to you, they have their reward in full. But when you give to the poor, do not let your left hand know what your right hand is doing, so that your giving will be in secret; and your Father who sees what is done in secret will reward you.

When you pray, you are not to be like the hypocrites; for they love to stand and pray in the synagogues and on the street corners so that they may be seen by men. Truly I say to you, they have their reward in full. But you, when you pray, go into your inner room, close your door and pray to your Father who is in secret, and your Father who sees what is done in secret will reward you [Matthew 6:2–6].

But love your enemies, and do good, and lend, expecting nothing in return; and your reward will be great, and you will be sons of the Most High; for He Himself is kind to ungrateful and evil men [Luke 6:35].

But when you give a reception, invite the poor, the crippled, the lame, the blind, and you will be blessed, since they do not have the means to repay you; for you will be repaid at the resurrection of the righteous [Luke 14:13–14].

There will also be rewards for our acts of piety and self-sacrifice.

Whenever you fast, do not put on a gloomy face as the hypocrites do, for they neglect their appearance so that they will be noticed by men when they are fasting. Truly I say to you, they have their reward in full. But you, when you fast, anoint your head and wash your face so that your fasting will not be noticed by men, but by your Father who is in secret; and your Father who sees what is done in secret will reward you [Matthew 6:16–18].

Notice especially Jesus' last recorded message.

Behold, I am coming quickly, and My reward is with Me, to render to every man according to what he has done [Revelation 22:12].

Finally, there is one category of people whose fate at Jesus' return we have not discussed. This is the group who are alive when Jesus returns, and, though they are not citizens of God's kingdom, they are not incorrigibly wicked either. These people will be judged together before God's throne, nation by nation.

But when the Son of Man comes in His glory, and all the angels with Him, then He will sit on His glorious throne. All the nations will be gathered before Him; and He will separate them from one another, as the shepherd separates the sheep from the goats; and He will put the sheep on His right, and the goats on the left.

Then the King will say to those on His right, "Come, you who are blessed of My Father, inherit the kingdom prepared for you from the foundation of the world. For I was hungry, and you gave Me something to eat; I was thirsty, and you gave Me something to drink; I was a stranger, and you invited Me in; naked, and you clothed Me; I was sick, and you visited Me; I was in prison, and you came to Me." Then the righteous will answer Him, "Lord, when did we see You hungry, and feed You, or thirsty, and give You something to drink? And when did we see You a stranger, and invite You in, or naked, and clothe You? When did we see You sick, or in prison, and come to You?"

The King will answer and say to them, "Truly I say to you, to the extent that you did it to one of these brothers of Mine, even the least of them, you did it to Me."

Then He will also say to those on His left, "Depart from Me, accursed ones, into the eternal fire which has been prepared for the devil and his angels; for I was hungry, and you gave Me nothing to eat; I was thirsty, and you gave Me nothing to drink; I was a stranger, and you did not invite Me in; naked, and you did not clothe Me; sick, and in prison, and you did not visit Me."

> Then they themselves also will answer, "Lord, when did we see You hungry, or thirsty, or a stranger, or naked, or sick, or in prison, and did not take care of You?"

> Then He will answer them, "Truly I say to you, to the extent that you did not do it to one of the least of these, you did not do it to Me." These will go away into eternal punishment, but the righteous into eternal life [Matthew 25:31–46].

In this parable Jesus refers to himself as the king who will judge the nations. He will graciously welcome those non-citizens of God's kingdom who have treated the citizens of the kingdom with compassion. (Judging an entire nation or people-group as a whole is not unprecedented since it happened several times in the Old Testament.)

Jesus affirms in this parable that there is an eternal fire. It was prepared for the devil and his angels, not for people. Nevertheless, it will be the eternal destiny of those who he determines to be sufficiently unrighteous.

7-11
SUMMARY

While it is interesting to investigate what the Bible reveals about the future of the kingdom of God, people have sincerely-held, widely-divergent views about it. Each person's conclusions are to a large extent based on what he or she believes about the nature of God and which parts of Scripture he or she likes to emphasize or de-emphasize. Although I did a tremendous amount of research both before and during the writing of this book, I cannot guarantee that the future of the kingdom will play out precisely as I have presented it here. God is sovereign and he is going to do what he is going to do. It is important that we understand and appreciate that. And it is comforting to know that we are not obligated to correctly interpret biblical prophecies that address the future. Peter excused us from that responsibility when he wrote,

> But know this first of all, that no prophecy of Scripture is a matter of one's own interpretation, for no prophecy was ever made by an act of human will, but men moved by the Holy Spirit spoke from God [2 Peter 1:20–21].

God will cause the big-picture events that he has foretold to happen as he has planned for them to, regardless of what we may believe or surmise about what is going to happen or how it will happen.

CONCLUSION

We defined the kingdom of God as his kingship and everything that his kingship involves, which includes his power, his authority, his domain, and his subjects. His power is unlimited: he is Almighty God. His authority is absolute: he alone is sovereign. His domain encompasses all of heaven and earth. His subjects include the angels and all of mankind. God's kingdom incorporates everything that is, everything that has been, and everything that will be. Each of us experiences joys, blessings, and privileges from living in God's kingdom.

Although the kingdom of God is one of the most frequently mentioned subjects in the Bible, it can seem complex and difficult to understand because the Bible is not organized topically. Instead, information about most topics is spread throughout it in a variety of ways and contexts. We investigated seven important topics related to the kingdom of God.

We began in section 1 with a brief history of the kingdom from creation to the coming of Christ. We gained insights into the reality and purpose of God's kingdom and the ways God works within it through studying his interactions with Adam and Eve, Abraham, Moses, and the nation of Israel.

The kingdom of God is a manifestation of what God is like and how he behaves toward us. People have many diverse ideas about God and what he is like. In section 2, we delineated the characteristics we would like him to have and looked at how closely those conform to what the Bible says about him. The two descriptions turned out to be remarkably similar. He is holy, righteous, just, truthful, trustworthy, and faithful. He is all-powerful, majestic, and superior to every other being yet is kind, wise, gracious, generous, and merciful. He loves us more than we can imagine, is fully aware of and attentive to everything that affects us, is approachable and available, and is minimally demanding. God is perfect, unchanging, and eternal.

Next we addressed our relationship with God in section 3. He allows us to control how distant or intimate that relationship is. But the closer we draw to him, the more fully we can enjoy the incredible blessings and privileges he makes available to us.

The most important aspects of living here and now in the kingdom of God are our relationships with God and with people. We addressed what our attitude and behavior should be toward fellow citizens of God's kingdom in section 4. Jesus summarized it best when he said that we should love one another. We looked in some depth at what that entails. Jesus also said that we should love our neighbors as much as we love ourselves. Based on that, we investigated in section 5 how to treat people who are not yet citizens of God's kingdom.

Jesus was uniquely qualified to speak authoritatively about the kingdom of God for two very significant reasons, which are explained in section 6. First, he was relating what he had seen and done while he dwelled in heaven before coming to earth. Second, he was revealing what he would do when he returned to his place in heaven, which would include reigning over the kingdom of God.

By means of his parables and what he taught, Jesus provided many new insights into the workings and the future of God's kingdom, which are described in section 7. He did that because the Father and he knew that, to the degree that we understand and adhere to those principles, our lives will be more fulfilled and enriched, and we will have a greater impact for good upon the people with whom we come into contact. We addressed many of those things that Jesus taught and how they affect us, both in this life and in eternity.

In conclusion, our responsibilities as citizens of God's kingdom are remarkably simple. We are to adhere to the primary doctrines of our faith, which have been summarized exceptionally well in the Apostles' Creed.

> I believe in God, the Father Almighty,
> Maker of heaven and earth.
> And in Jesus Christ, His only Son, our Lord,
> who was conceived by the Holy Spirit,
> born of the virgin Mary,
> suffered under Pontius Pilate,
> was crucified, died and was buried.
> He descended into hell.
> On the third day He rose again from the dead.
> He ascended into heaven
> and sits at the right hand of God the Father Almighty.
> From thence He will come to judge the living and the dead.
> I believe in the Holy Spirit,
> the holy Christian Church,

the communion of saints,
the forgiveness of sins,
the resurrection of the body,
and the life everlasting.

And we must adhere to the best of our ability to the three kingdom principles:

1)   Do what God says to do.
2)   Believe that God will do what he has promised.
3)   Then God will pour out his blessings upon us.

Finally, we must love God with all our heart, soul, mind, and strength; love our neighbors as ourselves; and love one another.

My hope is that this book has helped you better understand and more fully appreciate the wonderful blessings and privileges, as well as the companion responsibilities, we have as citizens of God's kingdom and that it has given you an enlarged vision for enjoying life as a citizen of God's kingdom.

SCRIPTURE INDEX

OLD TESTAMENT

NEW TESTAMENT

ABOUT THE AUTHOR

Eugene H. Lowe has three degrees in electrical engineering: a doctorate from the Georgia Institute of Technology (1970), a master's from the University of Southern California (1967), and a bachelor's degree from Louisiana Tech University (1965). Dr. Lowe has nearly forty years of experience in the high-tech world of systems engineering. His thorough and analytical approach to his work and life influences his writing and research. He has worked on projects for the United States Air Force, Army, and Navy while employed by corporations that support the United States government.

Gene was raised in the liturgical tradition of the Episcopal Church. In college he met Brenda, a Southern Baptist girl, now his wife of fifty years, with whom he has one son. Gene committed his life to the Lord in 1967, and both he and his wife were baptized with the Holy Spirit in 1971. That inaugurated a dynamic period of Bible study and personal growth that has continued to the present. Gene and Brenda have been members at various times of the Methodist Church, the Assemblies of God, and the Church of God.

Gene's relationship with the Lord is intimate and personal. He has a passion for knowing and fellowshipping with the Lord, for reading and understanding the Bible, and for worship through music whether alone, in small groups, or in church. This book is an outgrowth of his years of reading the Bible together with his continual fellowship with the Lord.

Gene has a gift for recognizing the most significant ideas in important subjects, and then presenting those ideas in a clear, inspirational, and easily understandable manner. He says, "My objective is much more than merely presenting biblical truth. My heart's desire is to present biblical truth in such a way that it touches the reader's heart and draws him toward a closer relationship with the Father, Jesus, and the Holy Spirit."

ADDITIONAL RESOURCES
BY EUGENE LOWE

To purchase additional copies of *Heaven on Earth, The Holy Spirit at Work in You,* and *Heaven's Success Secrets* contact HigherLife Publishing at (407) 563-4806 or email info@ahigherlife.com

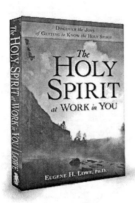

The Holy Spirit at Work in You

This book gives a wealth of biblical information about who the Holy Spirit is and the fulfilling relationship that you can have with Him. This book uses all of Scripture— from Genesis to Revelation—to guide you into a biblically-based relationship with the Holy Spirit.

Heaven's Success Secrets

This book will give you a look at success from God's point of view. As Dr. Lowe explains practical wisdom from the Proverbs, you will discover the importance of developing a personal relationship with God, dealing truthfully with others, listening to wise counsel, and other principles that will help you develop the right kind of attitudes and character traits that will lead you to a life of soulful satisfaction and true success!

If you would like to have Dr. Lowe speak at your church, conduct a seminar, do a media interview, or sign books, you may contact him at (407) 739-0516.

CPSIA information can be obtained at www.ICGtesting.com
Printed in the USA
LVOW10s0509260516

489840LV00003B/4/P

9 781939 183996